Adrian Burrows (b.1981) is an actor with a particular interest in ancient history and communicating that history through popular culture, film reference and the whimsical musings of his pseudonym Max Virtus. He performs, administrates and writes for Wicked Workshops – Provider of historical, living history workshops, tailored for KS1 and KS2 children, in schools all over the country.

Raised in Liphook, Hampshire, via Hong Kong, Adrian studied for 3 years at the University of Plymouth. Prior to this he gained a prestigious A grade in history for his GCSE... he then promptly disregarded history all together and followed his studies in performance and theatre. In 2003 love brought him to Lancaster, Adrian has since spent the past decade within the Theatre world as one of the founders of Little Gargoyle Ltd. Over the last 5 years he has taken Wicked Workshops to new levels of success, and thus his passion for history has been re-ignited.

As a freelance historical writer, his monthly blog for HISTORY IS NOW has been wildly popular and his writing has been featured in HISTORY REVEALED MAGAZINE. As a new father his most recent writing has been informed by late night and early morning gaming sessions of Farcry Primal, with the express purpose of an early history education for his young Son.

Though usually working within Wicked Workshops as an Actor and history practitioner, Adrian can often be found performing as part of After Dark Murder Mystery Events in performances across the UK. He starred in THE WOLFMAN INVESTIGATIONS Children's theatre production on its North West tour, including a run at the Edinburgh Fringe Festival in 2011. He is also one of the four cast members in the dinner theatre production THE PLAY'S THE THING, specially commissioned for the 400th Bard commemorations and presented by Attic Door Productions, (The production company behind the award winning HOW TO SURVIVE A ZOMBIE APOCOLYPSE). He has a brilliant rapport with children and spends several evenings a week running after school Drama Classes for children in his home town.

Adrian is passionate about ensuring that history remains relevant to people of all ages. Since becoming a parent he knows that history in all its mediums can be a fun and enjoyable family pastime.

His combination of broad shoulders and tiny waist means he has often been described as a triangle and he has a deep hatred of grammar and spelling – apologies in advance to his editor…

ISBN 9781911266280

Williams & Whiting (Publishers)

15 Chestnut Grove, Hurstpierpoint,

West Sussex, BN6 9SS

For Mini Max,

I'm sure you'll enjoy this once you're

old enough to read it

ADRIAN BURROWS

ESCAPADES IN BIZARRCHAEOLOGY

WILLIAMS & WHITING

Welcome Bizarrchaeologist!

Congratulations. By picking this book up, flipping it over to give the rear a cursory glance, then haphazardly rifling through the many pages until you thankfully discover that, yes, it does have pictures, you then decide to take it to the counter, smile gently at the wittering sales assistant, feel unreasonably guilty that you don't have a loyalty card, re-enter your pin several times in a PDQ machine that has an unyielding hate for small rectangular pieces of plastic, despite that being the very purpose of its existence, before finally stumbling home to sit in your armchair and dive into the leather bound book (not really, I think it's recycled paper) you now have in your hands.

Or you just downloaded it online.

Either way you have now been enrolled in the ancient and rather difficult to spell discipline of Bizarrchaeology. As I said before the incredibly long and grammatically suspicious opening sentence, congratulations.

My name is Max Virtus. Captain Max Virtus actually. I'm a Captain of Bizarrchaeology and your genial (and ruggedly handsome) guide to the underside of history. The weird, wonderful and just plain odd facts of the past that a Captain of Bizarrchaeology has pledged to dig up (I genuinely pledged, you can read the pledge on the next page. Let me tell you, trying to recite that bad boy from memory in front of a hall full of Bizarrchaeologists was not easy). For the last decade I have been unearthing the unusual and excavating the extraordinary. I have gathered together these weapons, armour, animals, stories, lessons

1

and ninjas and placed them in my Warehouse of Bizarrchaeology. And for you dear reader (and a small financial donation) I have opened the gates wide and am letting the history pour out.

So what will you find in this Warehouse?

For the ease of your navigation, I have divided it into several sections;

At the rear of the building there's the Zoo, cram packed with the weirdest events of the past that concerns animals (my cleaner, Phil, was attacked by a War Elephant last week so the Zoo has not been cleaned, I think the pages might actually carry some of that unspeakable musk upon the surface).

From the Zoo you can take a quick shortcut through the forest of forgotten dreams (not really, but corridor F doesn't sound nearly as exciting) and then you'll find the Gladiator Ludas. This lifelike replica of a Gladiator training school deals with all things Ancient Rome. And let me tell you, when it comes to those Romans, things get real weird, real quick. Enter the Ludas at your peril.

Over on the east side of the Warehouse (next to the snack machine, why oh why does it never have any Snickers*) you'll find a Pirate Frigate. The career choice of pirate has a long and convoluted history, I needed an entire ship to fit it all into.

If you leap from the frigate into the giant swimming pool that it bobs upon and head through the underwater tunnel, you'll soon find yourself emerging in my Weapons and Armour collection. This very carefully dusted section contains every single odd and bizarre way that a man has conceived of to kill another man. Just watch where you stand, I ran out of shelf space for the bear traps.

Over on the west side of the warehouse you'll find the Agoge, in here are all things to do with Ancient Greece. Just like with the Romans, when it comes to the Ancient Greeks things get real weird, really quick. If you then take a left and swing on the frail looking vine over the bottomless ravine, you'll find yourself in the Viking Treasure Horde. This section is jam packed (literally with jam, it's an excellent preserve for all that history stuff) with all things concerning our bearded Scandinavian chums.

Finally, at the front of the warehouse you'll find the Ninja Dojo. If you can avoid slipping over from all the wax on the floor (I tell that kid every day that its wax on AND off. He never listens) then you'll find many a fascinating fact to do with the Far East.

There are other sections of course but you're not authorised for those. Yet.

This journal you hold in your hands is divided in the same way as my warehouse. You'll find within each section a series of my Escapades. Oh, and there'll be a few surprises along the way too. You can read them in any order. Start from the front. Or from the back. Or maybe from the middle. Just don't read it backwards. That might result in you reciting an ancient incantation to summon a terrible demon from the 9th hell.

Well, what are you waiting for? There's nothing else written on this page.

*Other brands of chocolate are available. Just not from the Warehouse's snack machine. That only sells Snickers.

Bizarrchaeologist Pledge

To be uttered by the Grandmaster in a deep, gruff and gravel toned voice. Yes, a bit like the movie trailer voiceover guy.

Do you, Bizarrchaeotrainee, accept the 7 tenants of the Bizarrchaeologist order?

To respond I do.

Very well then let the tenants be stated.

To respond Let them be stated.

Tenant 1 Do you swear to forever seek out the strangest, weirdest, funniest and most interestingiest of all history and gather this information together?

To respond I do so swear to forever seek out the strangest, weirdest, funniest and most interestingiest of all history and gather this information together.

Tenant 2 When required do you agree to share with the world the strangest, weirdest, funniest and most interestingiest of all history that being the information which you had previously gathered together?

To respond I do so swear that when required I do agree to share with the world the strangest, weirdest, funniest and most intrestingiest of all history that being the information which I had previously gathered together.

Tenant 3 Do you promise that, if you really need too, you will protect, from the forces of evil, the previously agreed agreement to share with the world the strangest, weirdest, funniest and most interestingiest of all history that being the information which you had previously gathered together?

To respond **I do so swear that if I really need to I will protect, from the forces of evil, the previously agreed agreement of sharing with the world the strangest, weirdest, funniest and most intrestingiest of all history that being the information which I had previously gathered together.**

Tenant 4 Do you pinkie promise, whilst crossing your heart and swearing to die as you jump up and down three times on one leg, that you will protect from the forces of evil the previously agreed agreement to share with the world the strangest, weirdest, funniest and most interestingiest of all history that being the information which you had previously gathered together?

To respond **I do so swear that I will pinkie promise, cross my heart and swear to die whilst I jump up and down three times on one leg that I will protect from the forces of evil the previously agreed agreement of sharing with the world the strangest, weirdest, funniest and most intrestingiest of all history that being the information which I had previously gathered together.**

Tenant 4 And do you really promise not to tell anyone ever that there's only really 4 tenants and that we pretend there's seven so it sounds cooler and more serious and stuff.

To respond **Yup.**

Then I give thee welcome to the order of the Bizarrchaeologists. Go forth and third too.

Ninja Dojo

On entrance to my Warehouse of Bizarrchaeology (once you've scaled the moat and swum the wall. Inversion proves a formidably confusing defence) you will find yourself within the Ninja Dojo. For generations upon generations the Virtus family clan have been trained in the secret and formidable art of Ninjitsu. My father was a Ninja. My grandfather was a Ninja. My great great grandfather was a Ninja. My great great great grandfather was a Ninja. My great great great great grandfather was a pacifist so we try not to talk about him.

This is the first time that anyone has ever been allowed entrance to the inner sanctum of our dojo. Here you can expect to not only know how to become a Ninja but the secrets that even Ninjas don't know about. Turn the page and dive in (just not literally, that would result in you head-butting a book).

Shhhhh... Ninja Secrets

The Ninja really hoped no one noticed that he'd forgotten one of his swords...

Everyone loves a Ninja! I know that I, Captain Max Virtus, and the rest of planet Earth certainly do. But what do we really know about those Shinobi?

Not a lot. And what we do know is usually wrong. And what we don't know is mostly right.

The problem is that information is scarce due to Ninjas being so mysterious and secretive. Which was the whole point, after all they were the feudal Japanese equivalent of a Secret Agent. Each Shinobi was trained in espionage, sabotage, infiltration and assassination (although not necessarily in that order). Ninjas saw most activity during the Sengoku (or Warring States) period of Japan in the 15th century, which is when local lords vied for power and land, but had pretty much ceased to exist by the 17th century when Japan was unified. They were at the height of their powers for approximately 200 years, a drop in the historical ocean, yet we still fondly remember them today.

Now thanks to my warehouse of Bizarrchaeology, I have learnt a great deal about the ways of the Ninja. Sure, they more than likely spent a lot of time doing the things you would expect a ninja to do; setting explosives, tree climbing, making poisons, throwing shuriken and eating pizza in their sewer layer. But what are some things that you don't know about Ninjas? Glad I asked myself that question!

Ninjas love Cricket(s)

As I discovered when trying to sneak up on an owl whilst covered in bells (don't ask, I've set myself some fairly strange and highly unnecessary challenges during my time as a Captain of Bizarrchaeology) even the stealthiest of Ninja's footsteps can be heard. The best way to avoid this? Simple, bring a box of crickets with you wherever you go. Those chirp chirping chappies are heard throughout Japan, so a roaming Samurai won't be alerted by hearing their familiar stridulation (that's a fancy word for chirp but seeing as I had already used the word chirp in the previous sentence, I thought I had better use a different word. I wouldn't want to type chirp again now would I?) A skilful Ninja can release the crickets from their containment into the wild and then continue with their sneaking, safe in the knowledge that they will not be heard.

A Stridulating Cricket. Is it just me or would giant Crickets be freakin' terrifying? Let's all just take 12 minutes and 32 seconds out of our day and think about that.

Ninjas had fake feet

It makes sense, after all, the last thing you want that roaming Samurai to notice is a trail of footprints belonging to a highly skilled and deadly ninja. So instead Ninja footwear would have 'ashiaro' (fake footprints) affixed upon them, making it appear that the feet belonged to an elderly woman or a young child rather than a trained Ninja carrying a deadly Kunai (which was actually a simple gardening tool, it's going to look much less suspicious if a Ninja is caught carrying some hedge clippers rather than a skull split-tingly sharp Katana and a yumi long bow.) In actual fact, Ninjas rarely used the weapons that you'd expect them to (see the 'Time to Ninja Up' Escapade for a full Ninja weaponry breakdown).

Real Ninjas don't wear Black

Please note, these are not real Ninjas.

Yes, I know, I was shocked and saddened by this discovery too. When I think of a Ninja I like to imagine a man of shadow, clad in the distinctive Shinobi Shizoku, dressed from head to toe in an awesome looking black onesie of death (or a giant mutant turtle, either or). But that is exactly the point, the last thing a secretive Ninja would want is to LOOK like a secretive Ninja. Instead a Ninja should look like everyone else.

What would a Ninja have most likely worn? I'm glad you asked. A loose fitting Gappa travel cape that conceals light armour worn in layers beneath it (loose parts of the clothing would be tied with rope to prevent the total embarrassment of tripping out of a tree and ending up incapacitated in front of a startled would be victim). It's still worth wearing dark colours though, the last thing you would want is a red blood stain on your chest for everyone to see (Persil isn't going to shift that, I know, I've tried).

So there you have it, several things that you probably didn't know about Ninjas. Whilst reading this escapade you have also discovered how you can be a ninja. Because the best way to be a real Ninja is to be absolutely nothing like a real Ninja. After all that is exactly what a real Ninja would do.

So you want to be a Ninja? Get equipped.

You've learnt things you probably never knew about Ninjas and now you want to be a Ninja? Good to know (although I'm making a lot of assumptions there, but seeing as you, the reader, cannot directly communicate with me I'm just going to go ahead and do that. I'm also going to presume your favourite word is Philtrum). You're going to need to get the appropriate gear together. Don't worry I've got you covered. Here at the Warehouse of Bizarrchaeology we have a range of Ninja equipment suitable for a variety of sizes.

What do you need first? A weapon and the quintessential Ninja weapon would be a Kusari Gama.

'What? No Ninja Sword?' (I, once again, assume you shout out, startling the man next to you on the bus) Trust me, there's no better way of knowing someone's a Ninja than by them waving a Ninja Sword around (the clues in the name. If only they were called something else... like a Pinja Sword. No one would figure that out). Get yourself a Kusari Gama instead. It sounds fancy but essentially it is a simple wooden handle, attached to a chain which is attached to a sharp curved blade.

Most Ninjas would spend their time looking like simple Japanese peasants, which essentially meant having to look like a farmer. Therefore, what better weapon than one that can be separated to become a simple sickle and a chain? Two perfectly acceptable and non-trained assassin like items for a farmer to be carrying.

Need a long range weapon? Look no further than a flint lock rifle

'What? (I assume you've shouted whilst slapping your knee in delirious shock and spilling your finely brewed light ale in indignation.) Surely a Ninja would have a bow and arrow? Or Ninja Throwing Stars? You know... things that are silent? Not necessarily, whilst a bow and arrow would be handy, there's no actual historical evidence that shuriken were ever used in combat, and if they were, did a Ninja throw them, use them as a close range slashing weapon or as a zany earing? Either way, it's usually a better idea to try and kill someone from a long distance away so they can't try to kill you back. Ninjas would usually just be used in a spying role but if there has to be an assassination the perfect solution is a flintlock rifle. Ninjas were at the cutting edge of weapon development, experimenting with explosives and gunpowder, they would of course want the best tool available for the task they had to complete.

Chances are that if there were Ninjas today (obviously there are many highly trained and secretive Ninja clans in the modern world but if I told you that they might try to assassinate me) they would be armed with night vision goggles, cornershot rifles and red dot laser sights.

'I need more weapons' (I assume you bellow whilst stood atop a mountain wearing only lederhosen) then you want to get yourself a Jutte

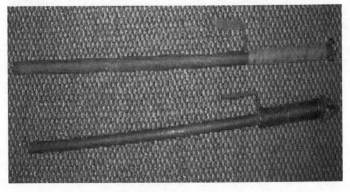

Originally used by farmers to remove weeds these little two pronged daggers were handy as you were legally allowed to carry them (back in feudal Japan only Samurai were allowed to carry a weapon). Not only that but the handy hook next to the main blade proved an ideal way of catching an unwary opponent's blade during an attack and would enable a canny Ninja to quickly strike back with a secondary weapon.

If you'd like to buy your own jutte then you can. A quick search of ebay has informed me they are available from many a disreputable seller at a cost of £27.80.

'What about if I want to climb a tree quickly?' (I assume you casually mention whilst circling planet earth riding a satellite). Then you'll want a pair of Shuko.

These are handy claws that fit over the owner's hands like deadly mittens. An essential part of any Ninja's tool kit were both easy to hide and enabled a Ninja to make a quick getaway up a tree (or to rescue a stranded cat). A skilled Ninja could also use the Shuko to block an opponent's blade, the advantage of using the Shuko gave the appearance that they were managing to do so with only their bare hands (not the hands of a bear however. I'm not propsing that Ninja's were half bear half man. But I think we can all safely agree that the world would be a much better place if they were). This served only to further their reputation as powerful warriors with Teflon hands.

But what was the most useful tool for a Ninja (I assume you state whilst hacking off your own leg with a spoon)?

That's an easy one. It was an egg. I'm not talking an ostrich egg here, I'm talking a regular, spouted out of a chicken, egg. The yolk would be removed from the inside of the shell by a small hole gently drilled into the surface. Then the newly created void would be filled with Metsubushi, a powder made of the sorts of materials that would make a grown eye cry. It's difficult to know exactly what Metsubushi powder is made of, as it was very much the decision of the Ninja, but one particular variety consisted of dirt, ground-up pepper, mud, flour, and ashes.

I wish I could tell you that a Ninja used the egg containing the Metsubushi as some sort of throwing device, ready to lob it at an opponent like a pyjama wearing Easter bunny, but if I wrote that it would be a lie, a beautiful lie, but a lie just the same. Instead the powder would be removed from the egg (which was simply a vessel for carrying the deadly powder that would not cause alarm if spotted. After all, it is a well-known fact that 84% of all people who lived in feudal Japan carried an egg with them at all times*) and then hurled at a foes' eyes whilst the Ninja made a quick getaway.

'I am sated. I now have all the equipment I require to level up and become a mighty Ninja.' (I assume you conclude whilst plunging head first into the sun with a fiery plume). Well good for you and good luck Ninja. You now have everything you need to make it as a Shinobi.

*Please note that this is not a well-known fact and has just been made up. Unless of course, you the reader, are of the philosophical disposition that there exists an infinite variety of universes and that, in one of them, 84% of all people who lived in feudal Japan carried an egg with them at all times. But typically in that parallel universe I didn't write this book, which would render this entire footnote completely pointless.

Make your own Mummy

I know, I know, you were reading all about Ninjas and stuff and suddenly Max Virtus interrupts to refer to himself in the third person and to talk to you about Mummies. Is this somehow a coherent segway that involves interesting historical facts about the mother of a Ninja and her remarkable skills of being able to cut pastry with a shruiken? No, I'm afraid not (although having a Ninja for a Mum or a Mum for a Ninja would be a great party story. Not that you could tell anyone your Mum is a Ninja, for all you know she could be lurking on the roof ready to slay every party guest with only a shoe if they were to discover her secret identity) although it does involve both my Mother and a Mummy.

Despite my efforts, it's a struggle to keep my Warehouse of Bizarrchaeology clear and organised. After all, you get everything all nice, neat and tidy, maybe even manage to polish an antiquity or two, and then suddenly a rampaging Viking Berserker is let loose in the Gladiator Ludas with a horde of human sacrifice loving Aztec Priests (from the Quetzolcoatl-Tlaloc Tlamocozqui sect no less) and before you know it all hell has been let loose. And a lot of water too, those Aztec priests know how to put in a good word with Taloc the Rain God. This sometimes means that things end up in the wrong place. One such thing is a 4000 year old Mummy in the Ninja Dojo.

Now don't worry, this isn't a Mummy with the power to transform Dwayne 'The Rock' Johnson into a strange plastic looking and possibly wipe clean CGI Man/Scorpion creature, instead it's someone who was mummified and left dead for a very long time in a sarcophagus found deep within an Egyptian tomb.

I tried to shift the sarcophagus back to the Great Pyramid of Giza in the basement of my warehouse (the real one, the version seen in Egypt is actually an elaborate fake, thanks to my great, great, great uncle Napoleon 'Virtus' Bonaparte for that one. He was such a joker) but even my mighty and rippling biceps and bulging pectorals weren't enough to shift that solid wooden mass with stone casing surrounding it. So it got left with the Ninjas.

However, in the process of moving the Sarcophagus I did discover a recipe for how to make a mummy from my mother, Marjorie Virtus. Now my mother is quite the character and spends most of her time in the dungeons below the warehouse investigating the most gruesome and gross bits of history. I've asked her to contribute some of her discoveries to this book, you might find some of them as you unleash constant pleasure on your eyeballs from reading all these words what I wrote (just hope the editor is up to scratch to correct the occasional mistake with past and present tense. I find I end up so fixated on events through time that I actually forget when the present is).

So why share the correct way an Ancient Egyptian would make a mummy? I'm concerned that people throughout the world will think that mummies are made, thanks to their experiences at primary school, by wrapping someone in toilet paper. This does not work. I know. I had my assistant Ian wrap me in toilet paper and whilst it was extremely fun (I pretended that I was Spiderman, if you pose just right it can look like the toilet paper is web fluid shooting out of your wrists. Top tip) it proved no benefit to the embalming process.

So read on and discover how you should actually make a mummy.

From the recipe book of Marjorie Virtus Page 5.

EGYPTIAN MUMMY

Preparation time: Approximately 70 days.

INGREDIENTS:

Dead Body (make sure they are dead beforehand, in my experience there's several ways you can do this but the best is to ask them. It always pays to be polite Max. Although sometimes if they don't respond they might just be sleeping. I discovered that at someone else's peril).

Some Pointy Sticks and a Stick with a Cup on the End (a gravy spoon can work great for this too)

Lots and lots of Natron (if you don't have lots of Natron just get yourself some table salt from the cupboard).

A sharp knife (I prefer to use a steak knife, and yes, I'm fully aware that we only have one steak knife in the house).

Scented Herbs (or use that old dish of potpourri in the lounge if you've nothing else).

4 Canopic Jars (again if running out of supplies I find that baked beans cans will suffice. Just take the beans out first).

Linen Wraps (don't use toilet roll. Used or unused).

Cedar Oil and Ox Fat (if you've none of that you'll find some low fat one cal spray next to the sink)

Palm Wine (if we're out I've got a bottle of Tesco Everyday Value Spanish Red* in the pantry).

*Editor's note: Other budget wines are available.

METHOD:

1. First of all take your dead body and place it in an 'Ibu' (a tent of purification placed near the River Nile). If you're not actually in Ancient Egypt, then any river will suffice although best to avoid one with any trolleys in it.

2. Then slap on your palm wine to prepare the body. Make sure you get it in ALL of the nooks and crannies. The alcohol content will help protect and preserve the body. Then you can wash them off with water from the River Nile (or the Jubilee River if you live in Slough). After all, they need to be squeaky clean for travelling to the afterlife. I prefer to use a loofah but the Ancient Egyptians would have used cloths made of linen.

3. Now comes the fun bit! Prepare to get your hands dirty (and by dirty I mean covered in blood and entrails) just hope your fellow embalmers aren't squeamish.

4. Get a chisel and stick it up the left nostril (the dead body's not your own). You then hammer the chisel until the skull cracks like an egg. You'll know when this happens because it sounds like this 'Kerrraccchhhhhhh'.

5. Then stick a hooked wire up the nostril (again, the dead body's not your own) and use it to whisk up the brain. Make sure you get a good bit of wrist action going and the brain ends up all nice and gloopy. Like a thick vegetable soup. A stick with a cup on the end is used to pull out the

bits of brain. You don't need the brain (according to the Ancient Egyptians it didn't do anything, there wasn't even a word for it). So just throw it away. Or eat it, if you're a member of the Papua New Guinea Fore tribe.

6. Now get that empty skull filled with Natron so that it doesn't collapse like one of my flans.

7. Next cut into the body (a nice clean cut to the side of the torso, just under the rib cage is best) and then reach in and start removing some organs. The liver, lungs and stomach and intestines can be removed. Be warned, there are a lot of intestines (each human has six and a half meters of them) so make sure you have a nice big bucket to slop them into.

8. Now get your Canopic Jars (you know the ones with the visages on the lids of the Four Sons of Horus). Not sure which organ goes in which jar? Let mumsy help?

• Imsety the human-headed god looks after the liver. You'll know what this god looks like because you probably look like a human too (unless you're some sort of evolved hippo with opposable thumbs, in which case ... good for you)

• Hapy the baboon-headed god looks after the lungs. Baboons are my favourite animal. Did you know that the collective name for a group of baboons is flange?

- Duamutef the jackal-headed god looks after the stomach. Top fact about Jackals? They can survive by eating grass.

- Qebehsenuef the falcon-headed god looks after the intestines. Strange fact about Falcons? Erm ... they can ... fly?

It's the canopic jar version of a police line-up

10. Once you've sorted all those Canopic jars just make sure you leave the heart in the body. This is because when the Egyptian journeys to the afterlife his heart will be weighed by Anubis. The better deeds the person has done the lighter his heart is, the worse deeds the heavier. If his heart is lighter than the feather of truth the person can carry on his journey, if it is heavier then they get eaten by the devourer (part lion, hippopotamus and crocodile—the three largest "man-eating" animals known

to ancient Egyptians) and then that's it. You no longer exist.

11. Now get palm wine and give the inside of the body a good clean out. Don't be shy, treat it like the dirty meat sock it is! Once you've done that cover the body in Natron salt to dry it out and leave it for the next 40 days. Just make sure you leave the body in a safe place, you don't want to forget where you left it.

12. 40 days in and its time to shape that body. At the moment it probably looks like a deflated air bed. Now is the time when you can get the linen, sand and herbs and spices to pad out the body. Do that person a favour, get them buff for the afterlife. Shape that body to give them a physique to make Heracles envious. Once you've done that, set your timer for 30 days.

13. Now, you've waited for a further 30 days, so it's time to coat the body in oil to make sure the skin is nice and flexible to allow for wrapping it in linen and give the body its distinctive 'mummy' look.

14. First of all wrap that head and neck. Make sure you don't leave an ear poking out. If you do it will soon drop off and they will be arriving in the afterlife with one less ear. It's like arriving at a party with the same outfit as someone else – but worse!

15. Then get all those fingers and toes individually wrapped before wrapping them all together like a big flipper. Don't forget your liquid resin (or no more nails will do the trick) to stick the wraps together and create a seal. Whilst you're doing all this recite some incantations to ward off evil spirits and make sure you tuck a few charms into the linen to protect the mummy on his journey to the afterlife.

16. Get those arms and legs wrapped separately at first. Then wrap them altogether. Don't worry if you're getting a bit tired now, you're almost done!

17. A shroud is wrapped around the body with a picture of Osiris drawn upon it. Make sure you use permanent markers so it doesn't fade

18. Then place the body in its sarcophagus. This can be tricky so ensure you get help from a friend. Why not make an event of it? Get a few friends around whilst enjoying drink and nibbles and chatting amicably about current affairs.

19. Now perform a ritual called the 'Opening of the Mouth' ceremony, allowing the deceased to eat and drink in the afterlife. Don't forget that. It could be awkward and they'd be the laughing stock of every other dead person in the Field of Rushes. The sarcophagus is then sealed.

20. Finally the sarcophagus is placed in the tomb along with furniture, clothing, food, drink and other valuable or useful items to assist the person in their journey.

There you have it. How to make a Mummy in 20 simple steps. Now clearly my mother was working with a very specific mummification process. The manner in which a person was embalmed would vary depending on their social standing and financial wealth. A Pharaoh would get the full spa treatment, whilst a peasant would be lucky to find themselves buried in a hole (worked well for Ginger though, he was perfectly preserved in the sand for over 5000 years. He was so well protected by the sand that even his hair, finger and toe nails were still attached when he was finally uncovered). Also the methods of embalming a body varied over the thousands of years the Egyptians carried out the process. I'm sure mother wouldn't mind if you varied things up by wrapping the organs in linen and placing them back in the body. You could even change where the sarcophagus is placed, after all, leaving it in a giant Pyramid for every tomb raider (Lara, I'm looking at you) to know it's there along with lots of treasure to steal surely isn't a good idea. Take a leaf from Nefertiti's book and use a tomb instead (no one's sure where her tomb is, though the current theory is that it could be hidden in a secret room behind the Tomb of Tutunkahmen).

Either way experiment, learn and most of all enjoy the time you spend with your dead mummified corpse.

Gladiator Ludas

Having exited the Ninja Dojo, it's a hop, skip and a jump to the Gladiator Ludas (it's important that you perform those movements in that exact sequence. Don't be tempted to skip, jump and hop, that will result in you being impaled in a pit trap large enough to perturb a Woolly Mammoth). The Ludas is a place to transform even the flabbiest of slaves into a chiselled death dealing machine of destruction. But don't just expect to find mindless violence for the entertainment and distraction of the Roman mob, the Ludas also has a senate meeting room for those of a more thoughtful disposition and a 5D cinema screen (which is an odd addition I must admit, Uncle Kevin Virtus was a little unhinged in his later years).

How to Survive as a Gladiator in Ancient Rome

In many ways a Roman Gladiator was a bit like a Big Brother Contestant. By which I don't mean that in the Big Brother household they are battling to the death with Gladius in hand (although perhaps they should be, Channel 5 take note). Instead I mean that Gladiators were both loved and despised, just like the fast fading celebrity who finds themselves in the midst of the Big Brother household. You can't help but think of the average BB contestant as being someone you totally dislike but at the same time you just can't bring yourself to turn the TV off (even when they've just spent the last 10 minutes screaming at someone for eating the last of the coco pops).

Gladiators were idolised. They were the sporting heroes of their time. A baby oiled titan. And yet they were hated in the same breath, they were slaves, and much lower status than virtually everyone else in Roman society (apart from the actors, they were the real scum). If you were unfortunate enough to become a Gladiator (unless you wanted to be one, free Romans were often drawn to the danger and excitement of the arena, although they would of course keep their identities a secret so as not to embarrass their families) then you had to work hard to survive. Balancing both being really good at fighting with having the charisma necessary to win over the crowd.

How did they do this? What top tips would they have shared in order to be triumphant?

Fortunately for you, I (Captain Max Virtus - expert in Bizarrchaeology – surely you picked up on that from the front cover of this book?) have the answer for you. I didn't discover this answer by reading dusty and forgotten text books or frantically scanning a Gladiator article on Wikipedia, Oh no, I LIVED the life of the Gladiator! Yup, in one of the halls in my warehouse of bizarrchaeology I built a miniature Flavian Amphitheatre, hired a bunch of highly skilled trainers and then I practised being a Gladiator. I did it all;

• Took on the role of a Venatore Gladiator and punched a hippo in the face (don't worry animal lovers, the hippo got to punch me in the face too, and they can punch hard).

This is the Hippo I punched in the face. He's called Hubert. Don't worry, we're best pals now

• Fought with a Samnite, Provocator and Murmillones Gladiator types, gladius to gladius. Practised using a lasso whilst training as a Laquerarii gladiator (don't try to lasso the hippo).

• I even rode on my war chariot as an Essedari gladiator (Unfortunately space was rather limited in my Amphitheatre, so this did involve a great deal of awkward reversing).

So what are the most important lessons that I learnt? What things can I share with you, dear reader, so if you ever were to be thrust back in time, due to a freak accident with an excited doctor and a DeLorean, and found yourself living the life of the Gladiator in Ancient Rome, that you could survive (perhaps even thrive) too?

Top Tip 1 - Never become an Andabatae Gladiator

Imagine the scene, you're a new Gladiator and you've just arrived at the Ludus (Gladiator School) for your first day. Suddenly, the biggest, baddest and brutalist (new word) Gladiator rocks up and starts hanging out with you. You are totally flattered because he is one of the cool Gladiators. He's then being all friendly and says something along the lines of;

'Hey dude, you know you would be major awesome as an Andabatae Gladiator. Would you like to be one at the next games?'

Don't be tempted, don't even pause to consider the question, just say NO!

First of all, I have no idea why the Gladiator was speaking like a Teenage Mutant Ninja Turtle.

Secondly, Andabatae gladiators were terrible, as your chances of survival were virtually zero.

To become an Andabatae you would have to commit a crime (this could be something major, like murder, or something relatively minor, like not being able to repay your debts) and then be sent to the arena to die. When you got there, you and a bunch of other criminals would be given;

A Gladius (things are looking up, a sword!)

No armour (that's not so bad, at least your opponents don't have any either)

And a helmet (yay!) with no eye holes so you are rendered completely blind (you what?!)

Once your helmet is on your head you would be sent out into the arena to frantically wave your sword around, hoping by Jupiter's left toe that you hit your opponent before they hit you. Even if you are struck by the pointy end of a gladius but end up only injured, you are still going to die anyway, because a friendly chap dressed as Charon (the ferryman to the underworld) will come along with a hot poker to check you're dead, if not, expect him to wallop you over the head with a hammer until you are (it probably won't take long, it's a big hammer).

Maybe you might get lucky and end up being the last man standing and get to live. But your chances are not even half as good as a regular Gladiator. In actual fact, most Gladiators had the best health care in all of Rome, with few battles resulting in death (after all, which self-respecting event organiser would want to pay out a fortune to the owner of the Gladiator if they were to die in battle?)

Top Tip 2 - Don't get the Emperor's thumb the wrong way around

So, you've just won your first big fight in the Colosseum with Emperor Commodus himself watching, exciting stuff! Your opponent lies exhausted at your feet and you stand above him, Gladius poised and ready to strike. The crowd chant from all around you in an incomprehensible wall of noise. You look up to the Emperor, he's stood there looking pensive (the lion's head he is wearing looks slightly pensive too - Commodus wore one as he desperately wanted to emulate his hero Hercules). Then with a nod the Emperor has decided, he extends his arm with his thumb pointed down towards the floor. You respond and with a neat swing of your blade your opponent is dispatched along with his head.

WHOOPS! You just disobeyed the request of the Emperor. You are in trouble.

Don't make this rookie mistake. A downwards thumb means let your opponent live (the direction of the thumb indicates that the blade should be lowered) an upwards pointing thumb means kill (the thumb is pointing towards the neck, where they should be stabbed).

Don't forget lest you really embarrass yourself and snatch defeat from the jaws of victory.

Top Tip 3 - Don't bring Kitchen implements to a Sword Fight

Being a man of wonder I don't make many mistakes (unless you count letting a Hippo punch me in the head) but one I did make was bringing the wrong weapon to one of my duels. My trainer had explained that in the next fight we would be battling as Scissors Gladiators. So off I went to the kitchen and fetched my finest Kitchen Scissors (they even have golden handles, to go with the theme of my kitchen) only to return and discover my trainer had a metal gauntlet on his right arm and attached to it were two large blades, jutting forwards like deadly trowel. It's then that I realised my trainer had said Scissores Gladiators rather than Scissors Gladiators. Suffice to say I lost the fight. Badly.

Go Forth Gladiator, Rome salutes you

So there you have it, now you will be able to survive as a Gladiator in Ancient Rome. With these lessons learnt you stand a good chance of getting your hands on the wooden sword known as a Rudis and earning your freedom. But don't worry, if you find yourself missing the danger and excitement of the arena once you are free, you can always go back to the amphitheatre for one last big pay-out. Just be careful, without an owner to have to pay a fine to on your death, you might find the event organiser won't provide you with nearly as good healthcare as before. After all, what better way for the crowd to remember the event than with the death of a famous Gladiator?

Terrible Roman Emperors

With the Coliseum fading into the distance it's time for us to find out more about the looniest people in all of Rome, the Emperors. But first let us consider some other equally loony leaders.

Every five years the people of Britain decide who to give the reins of power (I like to imagine that they are made from black flaming chains) to for the next five years. This means for six months prior to the big day we all have to endure (or enjoy – if you're weird) a constant barrage of political discussion (or name calling, hair pulling and a spot of eye gouging) across all forms of media and a forest worth of flyers to be gently eased through each letter box in the land. Even at the Virtus Castle I've had over eager enthusiasts from every party 'rata tat tating' at my solid oak door (this is despite the moat, barbed wire, an array of rock hurling trebuchets, a giant arrow shooting ballista and a quintet of flame throwing Pen Huo Qi devices, with enough combined power to keep Ghengis Khan and his Mongol horde away). I don't know why they bother; I can't even vote. This is due to the fact that whilst the Virtus Estate and Warehouse is within England, it is actually its own country, Virtusland (in the elections I get into power every single time), so this leads to a very disappointed (and possibly crushed, arrow pin cushioned and immolated) canvasser.

Apparently, in the last week leading to the big day, up to 40% of the people who have registered to vote are often yet to make up their minds who exactly they are going to vote for. There could be any number of reasons for this, but the one I'm going to focus on is that every single party leader of late seems to lack the sort of leadership qualities that enable them to convince everyone in the country to believe them. None of them come close to matching up with some famous leaders of the past who managed to convince entire continents that they were right and to do exactly what they said.

Could you really imagine the leader of the Labour party uniting the warring nomadic Mongul tribes in North East Asia and then going on to found the largest continuous empire of all time like Ghengis Khan?

Can you envision the boss of the Liberal Democrats ruling over both Upper and Lower Egypt, expanding trade routes and wealth over twenty years of peaceful rule and still find time to make the Nile flood and wear a fake beard like Pharaoh Hatshepsut?

Could you believe that the chief of the Conservatives would be able to forge an empire from disparate battling countries, have his accomplishments in human rights, politics, and military warfare remembered 2500 years after he did them and also to having a profound impact on both Eastern and Western cultures, all whilst he ensured that the Persian Empire was one of the most advanced in the world like Cyrus the Great did?

No? Me neither. Yet despite our current crop of potential leaders being rather dull, suspiciously similar (apart from wearing different coloured ties that is) and uninspiring, at least they aren't absolutely terrible, despicable, evil, cruel and driven mad by power (at least, I hope they're not). To look on the positive side of things I've decided to put together a list of the Top 3 Terrible Emperors of Ancient Rome, so that way you, the Great British public, can realise that you actually haven't got it that bad (Obviously lots of the Emperors did lots of horrible things to other civilisations but the listed terrible tyrants managed to ruin the existence of their own people with some impressive dedication).

You're welcome.

3. Emperor Commodus

Emperor Commodus liked to pretend he looked like Hercules. If only his lower torso didn't resemble a pixie kneeling next to a crab he might have been able to achieve his dream

Commodus, you cheeky chappie! Things started off all right because your father was Marcus Aurelius, one of Rome's most popular and well-loved emperors. You ruled alongside him for a while, which was a delight for the citizens of Rome, but when you became the sole Emperor things started to go wrong. You thought you were a god (always a bad sign) or to be precise a demi god, none other than the legendary Hercules (or Heracles if you prefer your myths Greek). You insisted on the visage of you, clad in the head piece of a Nemean Lion, be chiselled all over Rome on any statue you could find.

You also loved Gladiators and held loads of Games in which you often insisted to compete as a fighter. Although you rarely fought other Gladiators (obviously, they might kill you, apart from the fact that they were instructed to concede should they gain the advantage), instead you spent your time decapitating ostriches and killing lions (one hundred in a day, you must have got up very early in the morning. I barely have time to eat breakfast). You even fought and killed wounded soldiers in the arena to prove how manly you were.

If all that wasn't enough, you actually charged the people of Rome one million sesterces (a very reasonable amount you thought) every time you appeared in the arena. This caused the Roman economy to go into recession (yes, they even had recessions in ye olden times) and the currency to be devalued to the worst it had been since Emperor Nero.

Congratulations Emperor Commodus, looking after your massive ego at the expense of the finances of your nation and your people has put you in at No.3 on this list.

2. Emperor Caracalla

Emperor Caracalla permanently looked like he could smell a bottom belch (possibly his own, scholars are unclear on the matter)

Emperor Caracalla makes this list over some other truly terrible emperors (Nero and Elagabalus, you know who you are) due to the phenomenal amount of his own people that he killed. Caracalla believed he was a god (always a bad sign), none other than the brother or son of the Egyptian god Serapis (in fact he's the only Roman Emperor to be depicted as a Pharaoh on a statue). He also became obsessed with Alexander the Great, adapting his clothing, weapons, behaviour, travel routes and portraits to more closely resemble the legendary Greek leader. He even went so far as to assemble an Elephant division (rather foolish, as we all know how quickly an Elephant squad can be dismantled by a bunch of pigs on fire ... or you will by the end of this journal).

To start off his killing spree Caracalla had his brother killed (and all his brother's family and followers) so he could be the sole Emperor. He then had his wife exiled and later killed. He massacred 20,000 of his own people in Alexandria who didn't like the fact that he killed his brother (Caracalla claimed it was self-defence, the people of Alexandria then produced an amusing play to tease the emperor, he had the last laugh by murdering them for the insult). He then ploughed huge amounts of money into planning an invasion of Persia (just to be like Alexander). Eventually he was killed by a centurion when he had a wee at the side of a road on a long march (the centurion was angry that Caracalla had his brother killed – not because of the Emperor's shameful display of public urination).

Just goes to show that toilet breaks can be highly dangerous (hey, Jurassic Park taught us that but Emperor Caracalla's fate just reinforced it).

1. Emperor Caligula

As you can see this amphora of Caligula has some rather useful handles on either side of it, to assist in lifting the container and... oh... those aren't handles?

Where to begin? Emperor Caligula hits the Number 1 spot of the worst emperors of Rome for very good (or bad, depending on your point of view) reasons. Initially, once he got into power, Caligula was very popular. For seven months the people of Rome more than likely thought

'Hey, that Caligula, he's an all right guy.' Then things all started to go horribly, horribly wrong.

The shocking highlights of his tyranny include;

• First off Caligula exiled his own wife and then started to refer to himself as a 'god' (always a bad sign). He then followed that up by making his horse, Incitatus, a priest and consul. He even went so far as to spend public money building a marble stable with chairs and couches for Incitatus to kick back and relax on after a hard day of being one of the most powerful animals (including humans) in Rome.

• At the Circus Maximus Caligula became a little bored, as the lions had run out of slaves to eat, so to extend his amusement he had his guards toss the first five rows of the audience into the arena. Over 300 hundred people were turned into chew toys for the big cats.

• A man who insulted Caligula to his face was beaten with heavy chains. For three months. Every day Caligula had the man dragged from his cage for another afternoon of whipping. Eventually, once there was nothing left of the man and he could provide no more entertainment to the Emperor, Caligula had him beheaded.

• He even had an entire family publicly murdered, starting with the oldest so the youngest would have to watch it all before her own death.

His acts of cruelty, along with spending all of Rome's money on his own vanity projects rather than ensuring people had somewhere to live and food to eat, meant that Caligula's reign was a short one. In 40AD the senate were shocked to learn that Caligula planned to leave Rome and go live in Egypt where he hoped they would worship him as a living god. This was the final straw, and on the 22nd of January 41AD Caligula was stabbed 30 times by a band of conspirators. His body was left on the street to rot.

So there you have it, whoever is in power on any given Election Day we know one thing for certain ... there's no way they are going to do as terrible job as Commodus, Caracalla and Caligula. Probably.

Considering the vast majority of Roman Emperors were nuttier than a giant sack of nuts there is a very obvious question ... with that lot in charge how on earth did Rome conquer the Ancient World?

How Rome Conquered the Ancient World

The Roman Empire was, and this is a technical term so try to keep up, very big. Whilst admittedly not a patch on the rather stonking empire of the Mongols (Genghis Khan and his successors were kept very busy looking after an empire which had 22.29% of the total landmass on planet Earth) nor much later that of the British Empire (who ruled 25% of the population of the world in 1938, that's

458 million people number fans) the Roman Empire was impressive because whilst it only owned a paltry 3.64% of Earth, it did rule 21% of the population. Which means that 3.64% of land was where the party was. Not only that, but they managed it a 1000 years before Genghis Khan was out of his fur nappies (there is no historical evidence that Genghis Khan wore a fur nappy – but there should be) and almost 2000 years before Queen Victoria first gazed on Prince Albert.

How did those Romans manage this impressive feat? How did one city spread to conquer the known world?

In room 74B of my warehouse (take a left when you reach the land that time forgot but don't take a right. Whatever you do … DON'T TAKE A RIGHT! You got that? Right. No not right. Left) my intrepid assistant Ian, was tasked with conducting an experiment. Now Ian might not have a good complexion or an impressive physical stature but he is blessed with a lot of free time. He spent that free time in order to recreate an accurate and to scale model replica of the ancient world. It used up all of the paper maché in my warehouse (in fact we did have to utilise some watered down mummy wrappings to finish it off … sorry Hapsetshut and Akhenaten, my bad) but it was absolutely worth it when the intricate and finely detailed 3D map was complete.

Ian then furnished the landscape he had crafted with various models; people, buildings, villages, cities, rocks, trees, animals, and Darth Vader. Over the next twelve months he role-played everything that occurred in the creation of the Roman Empire. I don't know exactly what happened in room 74B (and I hope I never will), all I can tell you is that you could hear a handful of D20 dice being rolled long into the night. When Ian finally emerged, malnourished and bearded one year later, he had the answer. What did he discover in this carefully orchestrated and absolutely accurate historical experiment? Well, I'll tell you but I need to build up to it first. I'm going to raise the tension to near unbearable levels by first of all telling you what *wasn't responsible* for allowing Rome to conquer the ancient world.

It wasn't the Emperors

Let's face it, a lot of the Roman Emperors were a hindrance to the success of Rome. If an Emperor wasn't responsible for killing off the senate, torturing their subjects, engaging in some highly questionable and morally ambiguous pastimes, bankrupting the empire and then dying by assassination to leave a vacuum of power that resulted in a civil war, then quite frankly they just weren't doing it right. The various mad rules and actions of the Emperors often held back the progression of the Roman Empire.

Tiberius created a law that forbade any citizen from going to the toilet whilst carrying a coin with the emperor's head on. The punishment? Tiberius would break your legs (he probably didn't do it himself. It's surprisingly hard to break a person's legs. I only managed it when I fell off a medieval siege tower and even then I only broke the one. It was when the Mangonel misfired and launched a diseased pig carcass at my prone form that I broke the other).

Claudius had 35 senators executed, 300 equestrians killed and had his own niece Julia starved to death.

Nero made an even greater mess of things. He had his mother killed, along with multiple wives and lovers murdered and then even told Rome's Greatest general, Corbulo, to commit suicide (which being a duty obsessed kind of guy, he promptly did). After Nero popped his clogs (there is no evidence that Nero wore inflatable shoes of Norwegian descent, he probably wore sandals like every other Roman) all of his murdering shenanigans led to civil war and a rather hectic year for the citizens of Rome in which four emperors in a row donned the purple before promptly getting killed off.

Clearly those emperors really didn't help.

It wasn't the Roman Army

Yes, the Roman Army were very important to Rome's conquering of the known world. The highly trained and, most importantly, professional (getting paid to do something usually makes people more enthusiastic to do it) force swept aside most opposing armies that they faced. And if they lost round one they would come back and win round two.

It certainly helped that the Roman Legionaries had the best weapons, armour and artillery which ultimately led to them having the best tactics. This usually consisted of being incredibly hard to kill, hiding behind their scutums (just to clarify that scutums are big curved... shields) whilst jabbing at their enemies through the gaps in their shield formation with their Gladius (the best way to use a Gladius? Make sure you twist it when you remove it from your foe. It ensures their guts end up everywhere but inside their body). The Roman Army also had all the best toys as well, bombarding many a barbarian horde from a distance with their onagers (an awesome word for a catapult) and scorpios (like a big mounted crossbow).

The reason that it wasn't the army that was responsible for that massive empire? Well, they wouldn't have got too far without roads.

It was the Roads

Yes, Ian discovered that it was something as boring as a road that was responsible for one of the mightiest and long lasting of all empires. Roads, despite being a rather dull subject matter, were incredibly important to make sure that an army could get around the empire to keep it protected (and also allowed communication and trade around the empire to occur at a much more rapid pace).

Roman Roads were, as you would expect, incredibly straight. After all the most direct route from A to B is by heading right at it (although some Roman roads did run in zig zags to get up steep hills).

So there you have it, the tense culmination of this entire article was... roads. Thanks Ian. That was so uninspiring you've ruined Ancient Rome for me. That's great. That's ... great, Let's move on to a new zone of my massive warehouse!

The Zoo

Animals are weird. People are weirder. Combine the two and that's double the weird (which is four time the oddness and one fifth the crazy). With so much weirdness it made sense to find somewhere to put it all and that resulted in the construction of the Zoo. It's a vast sea of wrought iron cages spreading as far as the eye can see. A crooked forest of shadows that hides the most dangerous denizens of the entire Warehouse (it also has a fluorescent pink play park for the kids, it kind of ruins the spooky atmosphere but you've got to keep them occupied). It you're feeling brave, take the bundles of keys hanging by the entrance and jam them into the rarely oiled locks adorning each and every cage. Peel back the squealing iron door and peek inside. Who knows what you might find?

The Cat that conquered Ancient Egypt

First, let's start with everyone's favourite feline... but second, a diversion.

In the Armoury section of Max Virtus' Warehouse of Bizarrchaeology (Yes, as you are no doubt aware by now, I refer to myself in the third person. This only becomes confusing when I talk to myself) there are many bizarre and unusual weapons of war.

Which one should I share? There were so many to choose from... the 420 feet long Hellenistic Warships were an early contender (7000 crew on board? That's impressive. Also impressive that it even fits in my warehouse), then I had to consider the Byzantine Empire's flamethrower (they had the very first hand grenade too, all the way back in 673 A.D) and, of course, the Zhuge Nu Semi-Automatic Crossbow had to be an option (10 bolts fired in 15 seconds is nothing to be sniffed at). But none of those weapons had been responsible for an entire nation being conquered. The bizarre weapon I chose was accountable for such a feat. Responsible for defeating a nation that at the time was one of the most powerful and advanced in the world. A nation that we are still fascinated with today; Ancient Egypt. And most impressively the weapon in question wasn't technically a weapon at all... it was a shield. And even more impressively the weapon isn't even located in the Armoury, you'd find it in the Zoo.

What sort of weapon could this possibly be? Hold on, I'm going to draw this out a bit longer.

Invading Egypt was not an easy thing to do. Its expanses of near endless sand, lack of water and formidable armies had deterred many invaders over approximately two thousand years of history. The Babylonians themselves had tried to take Egypt by force twice and both times had been repulsed, so why did the armies of Persia think that their fate would be any different? The difference came from the cunning of one man and the knowledge of a culture's religious beliefs.

The Persian Leader King Cambyses II was well aware that the Egyptians revered the cat above all other animals. The cat represented Bastet, a goddess of home and love. She was both kind and loving unless she was offended, at which point she transformed into her alter ego Sekhmet the Vengeful and brought some divine retribution to those who had angered her (she loved the taste of human blood, probably describing it as 'full bodied with a distinctive aroma that assails the nostrils with a hint of copper and a bouquet of melted iron').

Cambyses had done his research on his enemy, knowing that to defeat them he had to find their weakness. He had discovered that in Egypt the love for cats was so great that the punishment for killing one was death itself. Herodotus the 'Father of History' himself commented that an Egyptian, if caught in a burning house, would save a cat before trying to put the fire out or try saving himself.

And so a plan was formed, I call it... THE CAT SHIELD.

Battle of Pelusium

So it came to be that at the Battle of Pelusium, Cambyses intended to deploy the cat shield. The Egyptians, under the leadership of Pharaoh Psammenitus (bless you), were feeling confident about victory, and why not? They were positioned in a series of fortresses near the mouth of the River Nile, they knew that their position would enable them to send down a storm of arrows on the Persian Army, perhaps enough to annihilate the force long before they had managed to join the battle. So, it must have come as a horrific surprise when as the Persian soldiers advanced they held aloft battle shields emblazoned with the image of Bastet.

The Persians, then revealed the second part of their plan, the soldiers released cats ahead of their formation, forming a protective sea between Persian flesh and Egyptian arrow. It wasn't only cats that the Persians had leading the charge either, they had, according to Polyaenus, 'ranged before his front line dogs, sheep, cats, ibeses and whatever other animals the Egyptians held dear' (just to point out that ibeses did not mean what I first assumed. The Persians had not managed to force a budget hotel chain to walk in front of them. Instead ibeses are long legged wading birds).

The Egyptian army, well-fortified as it was in Pelusium near the mouth of the Nile, was at a loss. They could not risk firing arrows at the Persian army less they kill or harm the animals at the lead, they could not charge towards the enemy as they would still risk harming the animals and angering their gods... what could be done? Chaos erupted in the Egyptian ranks that soon descended into a full route, and as they fled their positions the Persians pursued and cut them down.

Of course this being Ancient History, there are always historical holes to examine and question. The logic that protrudes between myth and fact. Primarily, if this is true, how did the Persians stop the cats from wandering off? After all, it's not like they would be able to train the creature to march along in front of the army. Different translations of Polyaenus' writings of the battle lead to different conclusions, some have theorised that the Persian soldiers actually held the creatures aloft in front of them, others, such as the historian Tom Holland, suggest that the Persians had a much more efficient and vicious way of ensuring that cats stayed where they should be … by PINNING them to the front of their shields. Here's the quote from Holland's excellent 'Persian Fire';

'When the Persians finally met the Egyptians in battle, it is said that they did so with cats pinned to their shields, reducing their opponents' archers, for whom the animals were sacred, to a state of paralysis. Victory was duly won. Pelusium, the gateway to Egypt, was stormed, and the bodies of the defeated left scattered across the sands.'

Regardless of whether the cat shield was simply an image of a cat on a shield or an actual cat nailed to a shield there is one thing that cannot be disputed. Egypt was conquered not by offensive weapons, such as a sword or an axe, but by the symbol of defence. By the humble shield. The Cat shield had been responsible for the fall of a country. The Cat shield had ended Ancient Egypt's sovereignty. The Cat shield had forever changed history.

The word Cat was said 23 times in this escapade.

Bat Bombs

The Cat Shield was an example of a defining 'weapon' in man's military history, a device that for better or worse forever changed our view on the world and our place within it. But it's not the only such weapon in the Zoo, take a sharp left when you get to the Bat enclosure and then I can present to you... the Bat Bomb.

First things first, I believe some clarification is in order. By Bat Bomb I do not mean the high tech compact explosive you would find on the utility belt of the caped crusader, no, I actually mean an incendiary device attached to a bat.

This idea came to be in the midst of the second world war and was the brain child of a Pennsylvanian Dentist named Dr Lytle S. Adams (Yes, that Lytle S. Adams, none other than the inventor of the fried chicken dispensing machine). Recoiling from the shock and horror of the recent attack on Pearl Harbour by the Japanese, Adams came to consider ways in which America could strike back at its faraway foe.

Dr. Adams knew that the vast majority of buildings in Japan were constructed from paper, bamboo and other very flammable materials. He had also witnessed the behaviour of bats during a recent holiday in New Mexico, particularly the manner in which the winged wonders found small crevices to shelter in during the day.

Taking into account these two factors Dr Adams had an epiphany; the results of this epiphany can be easily seen through a number of steps written as bullet points for easy digestion. I like to think this is how Dr Adams planned out his idea but there is no historical evidence to prove this to be the case...

TO DO LIST:

1. Get some bats.

2. Attach a bomb to the bats.

3. Drop bats over Japanese cities.

4. Bats spread far and wide before finally hiding themselves in the dark recesses of buildings.

5. After a period of time the bombs explode causing fires to spread rapidly across Japan creating chaos, panic, and destruction.

6. Back to work... 10.45am. Patient. Root canal.

It was certainly the case that Dr Adams' idea was unconventional, but there were top bods in the American government who believed that despite the oddity of using flying mammals as an offensive weapon that the theory was sound. That the bat bomb actually could work.

Adams submitted the idea to the White House in January 1942, where President Roosevelt himself authorised the further development of the project. It fell to the inventor of military napalm, Louis Fieser, to devise an effective bomb which was also light enough for the bat to carry. Fortunately for Fieser bats can carry more than their own weight in flight, so the bomb he developed was roughly the same size as a bat and was an impressively diminutive 16 grams in weight.

Now that Fieser had bombs attached to bats the next problem to overcome was to actually get all of them to Japan. And for this there was created an elegant and cunning solution. A device so simple and yet so genius I will write the details of it in its own paragraph.

A big metal box.

Yes, a big metal box with multiple compartments in which could be housed the hibernating bats. A parachute was stuck to the back so when it was dropped by a plane at high altitude over Japan, the descent of the box could be slowed. At 1000 feet the bats were awoken from the hibernation, the compartments then opened and 1000 bat bombs were released.

If at this point you are thinking that I'm making it up (and who can blame you), then have a look at the big metal box in question.

See! That's a big metal box, right?

So, how come the bat bomb was never used?

Well it was, only as a test admittedly, but the military were very pleased with the results of the bat bomb when it was deployed on a mocked up Japanese village built in the Dugway Proving Grounds of Utah. Yes, there were some setbacks along the way (the bats set fire to Carlsbad Army Airfield Auxiliary Air Base when they roosted under a fuel tank, resulting in property damage and a high death count of bats) but none the less the effectiveness of the bat bomb appeared to be promising. Not only that but bat loving mathematicians also surmised that ten B-24 bombers could carry over one million bats to their target.

So, to ask the question again, how come the bat bomb was never used?

Essentially the atomic bomb rendered it irrelevant. The new weapon was so devastating in its power and so terrifying in its annihilation of life that the bat bomb was consigned as a foot note in history.

So, how best to sum up? On the surface the bat bomb seemed like a ridiculous idea, after all, attaching explosive devices to any sort of animal seems like something you would watch in a cartoon. However, what if the bat bomb was used before the atomic bomb was dropped on Japan? What if this seemingly absurd weapon managed to bring a close to the Second World War? What kind of world would we live in had an atomic bomb never been used on a civilian population?

Let's leave the final word to the inventor of the bat bomb himself, when commenting on why his invention – 'X-Ray' - would have been a much better weapon to use on Japan than 'Little Boy' or 'Fat Man';

'Think of thousands of fires breaking out simultaneously over a circle of forty miles in diameter for every bomb dropped. Japan could have been devastated, yet with small loss of life'

We've looked at two animals that were utilised by humans in war (they didn't really get a say in the matter) but what about animals that took the war to humans? Don't worry my inquisitive friend, in the zoo we've got that covered to!

Emu War

'Virtus Nihil Timet'

That is the Latin phrase, carved in ancient stone which is mounted upon the entrance to the Virtus family castle.

It means 'Virtus fears nothing'.

There is nothing on Planet Earth that the Virtus family fears. Even if a member of the family faced in battle Hannibal's War Elephants, a warrior wielding a semi-automatic Nu crossbow and an angry bear riding a flying shark, it would still not cause a bead of sweat to appear on chiselled Virtus' brow.

But it's also not entirely true. I'm about to reveal to you, dear reader, the secret fear of the Virtus family. You see, that ancient stone should actually read...

'Virtum autem timet emu'

translated as...

'Virtus fears Emu'

I know what you're thinking, why oh why does the mighty Captain Max Virtus, the heroic adventurous dashing daring legendary darling of danger, fear an Emu? What possible sway could a big bird hold over such a man?

First of all, there are many powerful animals that have played a deciding role in history. The flaming war pigs that allowed the Megarians to defeat the war elephants of Antigonus II Gonatus, the war dog Sargent Stubby who saved the lives of many soldiers in the trenches of World War 1, perhaps even the Bat Bombs invented by Dr Lytle S. Adams (Yes, that Lytle S. Adams, the one in the previous escapade. You know, the one you just read. Unless you're reading this book in a random order, in which case... heaven help you).

But none of those animals have caused a modern army of one of the richest and most powerful countries in the world to SURRENDER.

Emus did. And they hardly even tried.

One day, my friends, Emus will realise that they are unstoppable and form an advanced civilisation that will ultimately destroy us all. Then they will form a new world, Emuopolis, in which Emus will rule over humans, who will do their bidding for fear of utter annihilation. This will allow the Emus to research and then build fantastic space ships, shaped like eggs, that will carry them to faraway planets until the entire universe fears their oddly proportioned shadow.

But I'm getting ahead of myself, how did the Emus defeat an army?

It's 1932 and 20,000 emus are wreaking havoc in Western Australia, destroying the crops of farmers during their annual trip to the coast. So the Australian government decides to send teams of machine gunners to cull the numbers of the birds. The name of the operation?

EMU WAR

However, the emus were ready for them. The large, flightless birds fooled the gunners by scattering and avoiding the hail of bullets time and time again. In fact, during one of the early 'battles' the machine gunners fired 2500 bullets and yet only 50 emus were slain. Regardless of the army's attempts to cut off, flank, and out manoeuvre the emus absolutely nothing worked. The emus were one step ahead of them each and every time.

In fact, the ornithologist (a fancy word for 'bird fan') Dominic Serventy commented;

'The Emu command had evidently ordered guerrilla tactics, and its unwieldy army soon split up into innumerable small units that made use of the military equipment uneconomic. A crestfallen field force therefore withdrew from the combat area after about a month'

That's right, emus broke the spirit of an army. In only one month. By running around and being emuey.

Once the Austrian army had run off, their leader, Major Meredith, commented on the military might of the emus;

'If we had a military division with the bullet-carrying capacity of these birds it would face any army in the world... They can face machine guns with the invulnerability of tanks.'

Let's just look at the statement ... and put it in bold font and capitals too ...

EMUS ARE AS TOUGH AS TANKS

This...

is as tough as this ...

So, that is why the majestic oak of the Virtus family tree fears the mighty Emu.

And that is why the ancient stone above the entrance to our ancestral home now reads;

'Vurtus nihil timet nisi Emu'

'Virtus fears nothing except the Emu'.

And now you know why.

It's important to note that Emus aren't the only animals who like to get involved in a spot of warfare, there's plenty of other beasts that would like to get to grips with the most popular human hobby of all... fisticuffs (or in these animals cases; hooficuffs)!

War Pig VS War Elephant

Ever since man realised that riding a horse into battle was much more effective than running on their own two feet, animals have become an effective and potent game changer in war. For Alexander the Great, the horse proved vital in carving out his empire in the ancient world. Alexander's 'Companian' cavalry would charge forward in a wedge formation, their manoeuvrability allowing them to be the hammer to the foot infantry's anvil and proving decisive in battles across Asia.

The use of the horse in warfare has continued to be seen throughout history, transitioning from its role as cavalry to the transport of artillery after the invention of machine guns (horses, unlike Katy Perry, are not bulletproof). But everyone knows about the horse in the use of warfare, in the Zoo, as you've noticed, we focus on the use of slightly more *bizarre* animals.

Pigs VS Elephants. Round 1. FIGHT!

Pigs VS Elephants. It would be an odd match up that's for certain, so first it's important to clarify why pigs would be fighting elephants in the first place. Around 4th Century BC (no one's particularly sure when) some bright spark in India decided that fighting whilst sat on an elephant would be a jolly good idea. Indeed, the general thoughts of Indian Kings at the time were that, 'an army without elephants is as despicable as a forest without a lion, a kingdom without a king or as valour unaided by weapons.'

The sheer mass and thick hide of an elephant meant that it could not easily be stopped by the spears of infantry (unlike the much smaller horse. Top tip, if you charge your horse directly at a group of stationary men, the horse will move to avoid them. French cavalry learnt that harsh lesson at the battle of Waterloo, when their horses insisted on running around the British Soldiers, who, stood in tight circular formation, insisted on shooting their rifles at the baffled horses and their befuddled riders), elephants can also reach a rather astonishing top speed of 25 miles per hour. Imagine, if you will, FIFTEEN elephants charging towards you at almost the same speed as Usain Bolt (his top speed being 27.44mph), it would certainly leave quite an impression on anyone in their way, both physically (and if you managed to walk away from it) mentally too.

This already formidable creature was then enhanced by weapons and armour. In India and Sri Lanka heavy iron balls were chained to the trunk of the elephants, which the animal was then trained to twirl and swirl like an overweight and angry baton twirler at the front of a marching band. Kings of Khmer utilised the elephants as mobile artillery, planting giant crossbow platforms on to their backs which could fire long armour piercing shafts at the enemy.

So you had 4500 kg of mace wielding and arrow firing elephant, what exactly could stop it? The answer was... not a lot; the elephant was the tank of ancient times. Even Alexander the Great respected the power of the war elephant, praying to the god of fear before going into battle against them for the first time at the battle of Gaugamela in 331 BC, and ultimately incorporating them into his own army as his campaign continued.

So how could a Pig possibly hope to defeat an Elephant?

The world found out during the War of the Diadochi, in which Alexander the Great's generals fought over his empire after the big man's death. The battle in question was the Megara siege in 266 BC, in which Antigonus II Gonatus advanced upon the city with a vast army, including a great number of formidable war elephants. The Megarians had to break the siege at any cost but how could they possibly hope to defeat such a mighty army?

Enter the War Pig. Just let that thought settle for a moment.

War Pigs.

Some particularly deadly war pigs would even use razor sharp metal discs (which they grow from their backs no less) to hurl with ruthless efficiency at their foes

First question, why even think of sending a pig to go and fight an elephant? The Siege of Megara was not the first time that it happened nor was it originally the Megarians idea to do such a thing. Instead it was Pliny the Elder (the Roman author, naturalist and natural philosopher) who determined that 'elephants are scared by the smallest squeal of the hog' which led to the Romans utilising squealing pigs and rams to repel the War Elephants of Pyrrhus in 275BC.

For the Megarians under siege, sending War Pigs out to attack War Elephants didn't seem nearly bizarre or dangerous enough. Instead they coated their war pigs in a flammable resin and set them on fire.

The War Pig had just become the Incendiary Pig.

The Megarians drove the flaming pigs towards the massed ranks of war elephants in a screaming, squealing cacophony of angry burning pork. Despite the forceful commands of the mahouts (drivers) sat upon them, the elephants bolted. They ran back through their own ranks, crushing both man and horse and effectively crippling Antigonus II Gonatus' forces in just a few moments.

The pig had been victorious. In the battle of War Pig VS War Elephant is was clear who the champion was.

So why did the War Pig not catch on? Why is it not known throughout the world as an animal used in battles and to takes its rightful place alongside Horse, Dog, Cat, Pigeon and Elephant?

The problem with a flaming war pig is that they have a relatively short range, about 400 feet, before the flames consume them and no one can resist stopping what they're doing and chewing on some crispy bacon. The other problem is that once you've set a pig on fire it's really rather tricky to tell them where to go (I don't recommend you try it at home as a barbecuing technique), there was just as much chance that the War Pig would dash through friendly forces as much as enemy forces, causing fires and chaos for both sides.

Fortunately for the armchair general, some animals are much easier to direct. Which brings us nicely to;

Pigeon Guided Missiles

Despite sometimes being labelled as a flying rat; the humble pigeon has often proven itself a worthy weapon of war.

Not the sort of weapon that you stab into an opponent, I would never suggest that a soldier should grab the nearest pigeon by the feet and flail it wildly through the air in a desperate attempt to sever his enemy's head from his shoulders (top tip, I don't think that's ever going to work). Instead, pigeons often proved to be rather useful in a subtler fashion.

All the way back in 6th Century BC, Cyrus, the King of Persia, utilised pigeons to carry messages around his vast empire and to coordinate battle strategy. This idea continued throughout history, taking on particular importance during the first World War. When pigeons proved vital in ensuring that officers had at least a vague idea what was going on in the mud soaked chaos of the trenches in the Western Front, thanks to the timely arrival of a winged friend carrying a telegram.

The Great War even led to heroic pigeons. The kind of brilliant bird that other pigeons could look up to, puff out their feathered chests and, with a pride filled trembling beak and a tear running from their beady eye declare, 'By God I'm proud to be a pigeon'. Pigeons such as Cher Ami, the Blue Check Hen who saved 194 US soldiers from annihilation by friendly fire during WW1 by successfully delivering a message to Headquarters, despite having been shot through the breast and leg by an eagle eyed German sniper.

Yet the pigeon's greatest moment was still to come, because during WW2, the American Behaviourist B.F Skinner decided to invent a Pigeon Guided Missile.

Yes. You read that right. A missile. Guided by a pigeon.

During the Second World War the American Navy were looking for a weapon that would prove effective against the German's dangerous Bismarck class battleships. Ideally something that allowed them to blow up the ships without getting particularly near to their fearsome array of cannons. Skinner's plan was simple yet strangely compelling, get a pigeon to guide the missile to the target. How would he achieve this incredible feat? Perhaps a tiny pigeon sized cockpit for the winged avian to gently slide into, grip the controller and declare 'toast me some bread I'll be back for breakfast' before activating his rockets and being sent hurtling to destiny?

Sadly, no, that did not happen. However, that didn't stop me from attempting it myself, despite constantly being inconvenienced by that small issue that pigeons can't talk.

First Skinner trained the pigeons to recognise and peck at an image using 'Operant Conditioning', a type of behavioural modification using both positive and negative conditioning.

Then Skinner divided the nose cone of a missile into three separate compartments and put a pigeon in each. Within each compartment were a series of lenses displaying an image of the target on a screen in front of the pigeon. The screen was cleverly hinged so that the pigeon's pecks on the target would affect the trajectory of the missile. Each time one of the pigeons pecked on the image of the battleship, the missile became a little more accurate, until it couldn't miss.

'It couldn't miss?' I hear you say (well, obviously I can't actually hear you, that would be impossible. Unless I were in the room with you, stood behind you, watching you read the word 'tapestry'. Don't turn around). No it couldn't. The brilliantly bizarre thing about the Pigeon guided missile was that it actually worked. Even The National Defence Research Committee were impressed, ploughing $25000 into the project. So what happened? Why hasn't this idea developed so that in 2016 we have pigeon chauffeurs, pilots and surgeons?

The problem was that no one took the Pigeon Guided Missile seriously, even though it worked, military officers were not prepared to be the one who signed off on a pigeon controlling a weapon with enough power to level a building.

Skinner himself confirms something that I've already written in the last paragraph 'the problem was that no one took us seriously'.

The project was briefly resurrected by the Navy in 1948 but by then the proven accuracy of electronic guidance systems was fast approaching and in 1953 the Pigeon Guided Missile was ultimately canned.

Clearly the world wasn't ready for a brainwashed pigeon trained to fly a weapon of mass destruction. But you're certainly ready to visit the next segment of my warehouse. Ladies and gentleman I present to you………………………look, I can't tell you here. You're going to have to turn the page to read the next chapter heading to find out. If the chapter heading went on this page, then the entire formatting of the book would be ruined. Plus, I'd make my editor cry … even more than he already is.

Weapons and Armour Collection

The crowning achievement of the Warehouse of Bizarrchaeology is the Weapons and Armour collection. There's so many items that I ran out of numbers trying to record them all. The entire area is filled with narrow corridors, secret tunnels and forgotten dust filled aisles and each one of those is cram packed with forgotten weapons of history. If you keep to the routes marked in red whilst exploring this labyrinthine maze you will be fine and will eventually emerge blinking into the light. Just don't follow the routes marked in crimson, maroon, dark pink, cherry, carmine, copper, fuchsia, magenta, ruby, rust, salmon, burgundy, scarlet, vermillion or puce. Following those easily distinguished colours will result in you never being seen alive again.

Iron Man Armour in World War 1

The First World War revolutionised warfare on an epic scale. Cavalry became redundant against the machine gun. The deployment of metal monstrosities, soon to become known as tanks, forever changed infantry's role in battle. The development of airplanes as weapons of war transformed the battlefield into a three-dimensional arena in which military commanders had to consider all avenues in order to finalise a strategy. The first use of poison gas in October 1914 forever changed our ethical and moral standpoint on the rules of warfare. All of these factors meant that officers on both sides faced a never ending tirade of new facets to consider when musing upon the defeat of their enemies.

However, this escapade isn't about any of these things. This might make you consider why they were written in the introduction to this column, to that I would give you two answers.

Answer 1: To boost the overall word count.
Answer 2: Tanks, air planes and machine guns were all successful in their development and use but that doesn't interest me at this moment in time, no what I'm going to be considering (and dear reader I hope you join me) are the military developments that were not successful. The ones that didn't take off. The genius ideas (and not so) that almost revolutionised warfare... but not quite. So what topic covers this remit? That would be Personal body armour.

Personal Body Armour

Quite frankly the headgear provided to soldiers at the start of the First World War was hardly fit for purpose. They either provided no protection whatsoever, such as the cloth French Kepi cap (which whilst it gave no protection to the head certainly made you look incredibly dandy), or made you a target (such as the German Pickelhaube helmet that had an easy to spot spike on top). The development of the British Brodie, German

Stahlhelm and French Adrian helmets over the course of the war cut mortality rates and assisted in reducing head injuries. So, some bright sparks considered... why stop there? If a helmet is good, then surely covering a solider in a metal suit would be even better! Or would it?

Brewster Body Armour

The Brewster body armour (named after its inventor Dr Guy Brewster) looked like a suit of armour crossed with a bear and was developed by the United States Army towards the end of the war. Whilst it was very clumsy and heavy, it could withstand the bullets from a Lewis Gun. Which was rather handy. The problems occurred due to the manoeuvrability of the person inside it being massively reduced and the small issue of the helmet not actually turning. Which, of course, led to visibility for the soldier on the inside being zilch. Added to this, the fact that the curved nature of the chest armour made it virtually impossible to grip and aim a rifle and you can see that pitching the armour to a solider in a front line trench would be a difficult proposition.

However, this didn't stop Dr Brewster from excitedly telling America of his invention. But being a man of both action and science (an Action Scientist or Best. Scientist. Ever) Dr Brewster didn't just tell people about his invention, he demonstrated it. An article at the time describes how the American military tested his armour by shooting at the suit whilst Dr Brewster was INSIDE IT. You would think that one or two shots would be sufficient to prove the protective qualities of the armour but that was not the case for the American military, who unleashed a 'rain of bullets' at the good Doctor. Apparently the military top bods were very pleased as no bullets penetrated the armour's thick hide. I can only imagine that Dr Brewster was very pleased about this too. At the end of the experiment Dr Brewster declared that being shot by a machine gun whilst wearing his armour was only about 'one tenth the shock which he experienced when struck by a sledge-hammer.' One has to wonder how he knew what it felt like to be hit by a sledge-hammer.

Unfortunately for Dr Brewster his body armour never took off, the American Military choosing not to utilise it in the field. This always struck me as a shame for after all, surely the Brewster Armour was a precursor to a real life Iron Man suit (let's face it, we've all been waiting for one and the fact that's it's now 2016 and no-one's invented it yet is frankly shocking) *.

Clearly the Brewster armour was unsuitable for the requirement of life in the trenches and warfare across no man's land. Just the additional weight of the armour alone would make traversal of mud and hazard strewn terrain effectively impossible. Yet there is still some fascinating theorising that suggests if body armour was provided to soldiers then thousands of lives could have been saved.

The majority of injuries to soldiers in the First World War were caused by shrapnel to the chest and head, not bullets and poison gas. Surely if a soldier could protect these areas then their chances of survival would be drastically increased? The Brewster armour was ridiculous in many ways, yet at its core Dr Brewster had a very pure desire, to keep soldiers alive. Unfortunately, over the four years of the First World War very little developments were made in the field of body armour, it took a good two years for most soldiers to get a metal helmet rather than a cloth cap. Perhaps if someone had managed to design and mass produce effective body armour then hundreds of thousands of lives could have been saved by the end of the war.

*And whilst I'm at it, where is my hover skateboard? I'm looking accusingly at your false promises Back to the Future II.

Top 3 Weirdest Tanks. Ever.

Since we've been talking the Great War, it's common knowledge that since that conflict, the mighty tank has formed the mainstay of any skilled (or unskilled) military commander's army in the modern age. The tank started its military career from fairly inauspicious beginnings. Originally called 'Landships' (this name didn't stick as military bods were concerned that such an overly descriptive title might give away what their secret weapon was to the enemy, so the name 'tank' was instead adopted) the tank really hasn't changed a great deal in its design or function since its first use in battle. Yes, advances in technology have rendered a modern tank a distance relative to the first tank prototype (fondly named as 'Little Willie' by the British Military) but it still remains a relative none the less.

The classic image of a tank is of a hulking, box like central chassis, the twin caterpillar tracks placed on either side in order to propel its vast form forward over any and all terrain, and a rotating turret to provide a 360-degree field of fire. Perhaps the core tenants of the tank design haven't changed, because the initial concept was just so effective. Why try to fix what isn't broken? Well, that didn't stop people from trying. And try they did. My Warehouse is crammed with their successes (those with less imagination might call these inventions failures, to myself they are glorious triumphs in the bizarre) allow me to share with you my favourite three. My top three if you will.

The Tsar Tank in all its Penny-Farthing glory

3: The Russian Tsar Tank

Caterpillar tracks are brilliantly effective at moving big heavy tanks across difficult terrain. Indeed, they were initially designed in order to allow tanks to climb up and over the trench laden terrain of the Western Front. Yet, as thought by the Russian boffins Nikolai Lebedenko, Nikolai Zhukovsky, Boris Stechkin and Alexander Mikulin, if caterpillar tracks are great then surely two giant bicycle wheels would be awesome.

That was the primary design decision behind the Russian Tsar Tank and what a sight it was. Each giant spoked wheel attached to the central hub of the chassis was a massive 27 feet in diameter, the idea being that such a vast wheel would be able to plough through any obstacles in its path (and the two 250 hp Sunbeam engines would certainly help with that). The tank was ready for war armed with a giant 8-metre-high cannon turret and plans for further cannons to be attached to the tank's frame. The central casing itself was a massive 12 metres wide with thick armour to protect the soldiers inside. So far so good right? Surely no other tank could withstand the might of this creation? Why on earth didn't the Russian Tsar tank take off?

Its Achilles heel turned out to be the small stabilising wheel at the rear of the tank (giving it its tricycle appearance). During the first test run through a field, the stabilising wheel became firmly entrenched in a patch of mud. The entire mighty form of the Tsar Tank became rooted to the spot, making it a big target that resembled a giant penny farthing. After the abysmal test run the tank never saw active service and remained stuck exactly where it was until the end of the war. Fortunately, that very tank ended up in my warehouse.

2: Ball Tank

Texan Inventor AJ Richardson had a noble goal, how best to ensure men could quickly and safely cover the distance of a mud and crater strewn no man's land in order to close in on an enemy position? The answer he came up with? A giant metal ball. This mighty metal ball of death could not only protect the troops within but, being spherical, it could also outmanoeuvre anything else on the battlefield. The project never was developed due to one small problem that scientists at the time could not overcome... there was no way that the troops within could see outside of the tank. In theory though it would have been amazing.

Is it a bird? Is it a plane? No, it's a flying tank!

1: Antonov A-40 Krylya Tanka (Tank Wings)

Tanks are big and powerful but slow and cumbersome. If somehow their manoeuvrability could be increased, then surely nothing could stand in their path as they rapidly out flanked the enemy's position. The logical conclusion to this quandary? Invent a tank that can fly.

And that's exactly what Oleg Antonov set about doing in 1942. A T-60 Light tank (light being 5.8 tonnes) went on a crash diet under Antonov's watchful eye by removing the vehicle's armour, weaponry and headlights. The T-60 was also provided with a limited amount of fuel in order to decrease its total weight yet further. What was the next step? Attach some wings to the tank of course. Yes, they were literally stuck to the side of the tank, transforming it into the world's most unlikely glider. Final step was to utilise a Tupolev TB-3 plane to lift the tank gently in to the air, once the plane had reached a sufficient height and speed the prototype could be released, allowing it to glide majestically into battle.

Did it work? I would love to say yes, but no, no it didn't.

Remarkably no one died in the experiment, the TB-3 had to ditch the tank in mid-flight due to the massive drag it caused, but apparently the T-60 did glide back down to earth before being driven back to base. This initial set back didn't put off the Soviet Union though, over the next twenty years they were able to develop the necessary techniques and equipment to para-drop BMD-1 vehicles with their crew ON BOARD.

At this escapade clearly demonstrated, I really like Top 3 lists and what's one better that a Top 3 List? A Top 4 list of course. Which neatly brings us to

The 4 Most Awesome Swords. Ever.

There are three things in this world that are true. The Sun is hot. Water is wet... and swords are awesome. As I sit here in the sword wing of my Warehouse of Bizarrchaeology, I find myself gazing over racks and racks of blades and I start to consider... which of these are the Top 4 Most Awesome Swords. EVER (everyone does a Top 5 or a Top 10, I'm going for a Top 4).

This is tricky, after all there are so many swords in my warehouse to consider. In one of the boxes I have one of Napoleon's swords (I paid a mere $6.4 million dollars for it back in 2007, it's rather pleasant, the blade is gold encrusted and looks great but highly ineffective at completing basic sword requirements. Like chopping off limbs. Don't ask me how I know this, suffice to say it took a lot of super glue to put both the sword and the limb back together). Then there is the rather impressive 132cm long sword that belonged to the Scottish Hero, William Wallace, surprisingly dubbed the Wallace Sword. Not to forget the rather impressive Tizona, the beautiful blade made of Damascus steel that the Spanish Hero El Cid used to battle the Moors. But none of these blades were strange enough to belong in an Escapade in Bizarrchaeology. So that's why I settled on the following bizarrely brilliant weapons.

4. Khopesh Sword

The Ancient Egyptian Khopesh Sword is based on one simple question, why have a sword or an axe when you can have both? And thanks to King Eannatum of Lagash who was the first to give this weapon a go back in 2500 BC, now you can. At its hilt the Khopesh resembled a broad sword, yet rather than the blade running in a straight line to its tip, it instead curls back on itself like a crook, this caused the weapon to resemble a leg of beef (which is where its name derives from). The Khopesh was rather short at 24 inches long but the blunted end proved very effective at being used as a hook to surprise an unwitting opponent. The Khopesh sword was incredibly popular and was an Egyptian warrior's weapon of choice and must have fashion accessory for close to 1200 years. It was also very effective at hair crimping. Fact.

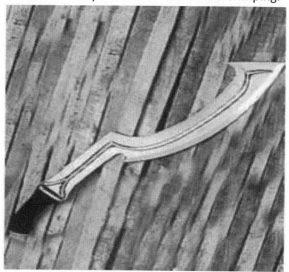

No scabbard could possibly contain the seven branch sword

3. Seven - Branch Sword

Why settle for one, two, three, four, five or six blades on your sword when you can have seven? That's a motto to live your life by and that's exactly what the Baekje Dynasty, in Ancient Korea around 372 AD, did when they constructed this mightily impressive and over bearingly bladey Seven Branch Sword. This weapon was never intended for battle and was instead built for ceremonial purposes. But having sharpened up the Iron blade and swinging it around a bit I can assure you that it is highly effective at chopping seven melons in half. AT THE SAME TIME. It made preparing the starter for my last dinner party an absolute doddle!

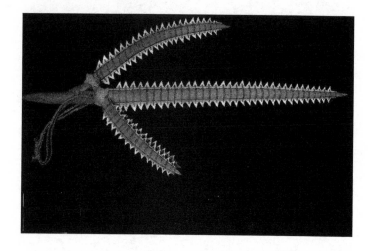

2. Shark Tooth Sword

Some weapons just make sense. If you're going to make a sword, then make it with shark teeth. First off, sharks have up to 20,000 teeth, whenever they lose one, another grows to take its place. That means there's a lot of shark teeth floating around the ocean to turn into a sword. And that's exactly what the denizens of the Gilbert Island of Kiribati decided to do. Shark Tooth weapons have been made in the 16 Gilbert islands for generations, everything from shark tooth spears, to daggers and even knuckle dusters are created. The above Shark Tooth sword is a three-pronged blade with 100 shark teeth mounted on coconut wood and held in place with twine and human hair. It's almost the most awesome sword ever devised by human mind. Almost.

So...many...swords...

1. Urumi Swords

The problem with using a sword in battle is that it can be rather restrictive, it has a specific length of blade that only has a certain attack distance. This does not apply to the Urumi Swords and that is precisely what makes the Urumi Swords so phenomenally awesome. Imagine a sword crossed with a Slinky and you have a Urumi Sword (get back on your feet once you've recovered from the sheer awesomeness of that statement and continue reading). Developed in the Southern States of India during the Maurya Dynasty, this bladed whip like sword can only be used by an expert trained in the Indian Martial Arts. Why? Well, the danger is that as you flail around with this giant extendible sword you might accidentally cut your own face off. Which believe me you would not want to do (to fix this would require even more super glue than repairing Napoleon's sword).

The standard Urumi consists of only one blade that is four to five feet long, however, the Sri Lankan version has up to THIRTY TWO blades attached to one handle. Not only that but the warrior would fight with one Urumi in each hand, leading to SIXTY FOUR blades whizzing around the place.

And the best thing about the Urumi? After you've finished the swings, spins and turns that make up the attack pattern you can wear the Urumi around your waist like a belt. Which surely must be the best belt ever. So not only is the Urumi the most awesome sword ever it is the most awesome belt ever too.

*Whilst this list was called the Top 4 most awesome swords, EVER, it did not include swords which haven't been invented yet, otherwise this list would have obviously contained a Lightsaber.

By now you're probably thinking to yourself 'Hey, I really hope this Max Virtus guy doesn't do another Top 3 or Top 4 or even Top 5 list, otherwise I'll start to become concerned that this book is becoming slightly repetitious'. To that I'd reply 'Uh oh'.

Top 4 Most Awesome Guns. Ever.

1011 words ago I gently eased open the creaky door to the Sword Armoury in my Warehouse of Bizarrchaeology. We had some fun, we waved some swords and learnt a little more about each other. In the process of all these sword related shenanigans it got me thinking. Thinking about guns.

After all, even the most awesome sword ever would prove ineffectual against a Bazooka (unless you are a Space Samurai and can slice through the rocket using your adamantium blade and use the resulting explosion to catapult yourself in dramatic slow motion through the air to embed your sword in to your opponent. If not, you're always going to lose against a guy with a bazooka).

The problem is that most guns are a bit... boring. You need only see a few AMT Automag IIIs, a smattering of Astra 400s and a soupçon of Ballester-Molinas before they all look like just another thing that goes 'shooty shooty bang bang' and you find yourself wishing for a 32 bladed Urami sword.

So which guns buck the boring trend? Which guns are the Most AWESOME Guns in History? Let's find out!

Pen Pistol

This is just a regular pen. Or is it? That's the beauty of a Pen Pistol, you won't know for sure until you end up shot or covered in ink

Have you ever been stuck in an office wishing your pen was a gun? Perhaps your boss just slapped down on your desk a thick wad of paperwork, along with strict instructions that every sheet must be signed off before you are finally allowed to escape the wretched cubicle that has been your home for the last ten hours. Then wish no longer, simply retrieve your R.J. Braverman Stinger Pen Pistol from your Pikachu shaped pen pot, slide it open and fold the 5.5-inch shaped wonder in the middle, so that it is primed and ready to fire. Now you can ensure that your boss will be letting you go home and will also provide you with a lift. And a bonus. And a Squirtle shaped pen pot.

Duckfoot Pistol

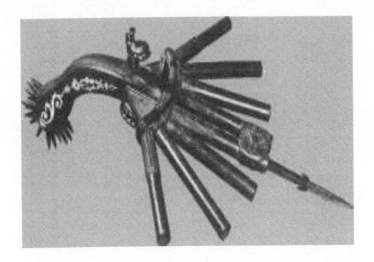

If this is what a Duck's foot look like, then that's a very ill duck

In the 18th Century guns had one major flaw. Their reload time was ridiculously slow. Having to painstakingly prime and load after each shot, then needing to use a ram rod to push the pistol shot into position, before finally able to fire a volley at the angry man running straight towards you waving an axe enthusiastically above his head, was not a great way of increasing your survival chances on the battlefield.

Which is why some bright spark (their name has been lost in the annals of history but I think they could well be called Jeff. Jeff Spark) decided to take the basic idea of a Volley Gun (that being a very big gun with multiple barrels secured to a wheeled carriage) and combine it with a pistol to create the seven barrelled delight that you see above you. Whilst the recoil caused by firing multiple bullets at once would have been extremely unpleasant, the weapon proved rather effective for those fighting at close quarters against multiple opponents.

The design was taken to the extreme by Giuseppe Marco Fieschi, who in June 1835, used a home-made, 25-barrel volley gun to attempt to assassinate the French King Louis Philippe I. He called it the *Machine infernale*. The would-be assassin fired his custom weapon from a third story window at the King, who was unaware below. Whilst managing to kill 18 people, Guiseppe only managed to scratch the King and was unable to perform a daring escape as four of the gun's barrels had exploded, ensuring that he was easily caught and guillotined the following year.

Oh, and the gun was called a Duck Foot as its four barrels and rear stock made it look like the flipper of a pond visiting quacker.

Sword Gun

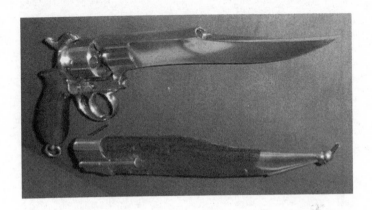

If you look at this Sword Gun too long it starts to look incredibly phallic. And once you've noticed that, it can't be unseen

Do you find yourself waking up in the middle of the night in a cold sweat, frantically trying to choose between having a sword or a gun as your favourite weapon? Is your mind in a tight knot as you consider the benefits of each weapon? Then you need panic no longer. Don't choose between a sword or gun. Get yourself a handy sword gun instead.

Whilst there are a surprisingly large number of Sword Guns invented over the years the most amazing would have to be the Swedish 'Cutlass Pistol'. Surely the dream weapon of any Golden Age Pirate. Devised in 1865 by the Swedish Government the Cutlass Pistol was intended to be used by prison guards, as it was ideal for close quarters combat but was absolutely useless when attempting to inflict stabby or shooty pain on anyone more than a few paces from the wielder. I know that, as I have my own Cutlass Pistol and trying to aim the thing is ridiculously difficult, in fact, during the test shots I managed to hit everything in the room (including myself... don't ask) except what I was actually trying to aim for. The Cutlass Pistol didn't even make for a particularly effective sword, as the weight of the gun ruined the balance of the weapon, making it difficult to parry and thrust faster than your opponent (which is essentially what sword fighting comes down to, despite what Hollywood wants you to think, all you need to do is jab your weapon into your enemy quicker than they can jab it into you. No rope swinging, back flipping or spinning required). So the Sword Gun was a failed experiment, but what a GLORIOUS failed experiment it was!

Cemetery Gun

Here's a cemetery. No gun. Just the cemetery. It's a little depressing I'll be honest with you

The Cemetery Gun would be used in the exact location its name would suggest; graveyards. It was invented in the 18th century, which makes you wonder if there was some sort of freak Zombie outbreak during the time, that was later hushed up by the sinister and black polo neck wearing powers that be (9 out of 10 evil villains prefer a polo neck over any other jumper). The gun would be placed next to a grave (it was fairly small, with a barrel of only 9 inches long, making it easy to hide in a shrub of grass or a bush) and was activated by one of three nearby wires being tripped. Surely the only purpose for this would be to ensure that any member of the rising dead get a bullet to the head as they emerge into the world?

Not entirely (although when the apocalypse finally comes I'm expecting the cemetery gun to be back in fashion. It would solve all their problems in 'The Walking Dead'. As, to be fair, would some cold weather), during the 18th and 19th centuries grave robbing was a very well paid profession. Medical students struggled to get their hands legally on a cadaver, so the ambitious robber could make himself a lot of money very quickly. And they would never run out of dead bodies to steal, which is surely the best blue ocean thinking ever. However, from 1810 onwards the cemetery gun soon proved an effective deterrent, after all, who wants to be shot in the ankle? Only people who hate their ankles, that's who.

Ironically medical students were allowed to perform autopsies on the dead bodies of criminals, so the unwitting Grave Robber could provide the requested product, just not in the way they were expecting.

The Grave Robbers were pretty canny though and disguised themselves as women in mourning so they could visit the graveyard during the day and suss out where the guns had been positioned. Cemetery Keepers combated this by only placing the cemetery guns at night. The conflict between Grave Robber and Cemetery Keeper escalated like nuclear deterrents between rival super powers. Who would win? Neither in the end. When the legalities of performing dissections on corpses were changed to favour scientists, the grave robber was no longer needed and nor was the Cemetery Gun (until the Zombie apocalypse that is).

Are you as bored of Top [insert number of your choice here list] lists as I am now we've had 3? Yes? Then let's do something different. How about I tell you about the time I test drove a dangerous weapon?

Cannon Scooter Test Drive

Whilst my collection of Bizarrchaeology items within my secret warehouse is vast, every now and again I find a hole in my compilation.

Last Tuesday was one such day. I learnt that my collection was missing a cannon scooter.

Yes, a CANNON SCOOTER.

Now for those of you not back flipping with joy at this moment in time, allow me to reassert what a cannon scooter is;

It's a scooter with a giant cannon attached to it

Just imagine riding this vehicle, the wind blowing in your hair, maybe your cape billowing behind you, using the mighty cannons to shoot obstacles out of the way.

How had this beautiful vehicle been missing from my life? How was I not even aware that some genius inventor had taken the entirely logical step of attaching a massive piece of military hardware to the equivalent of a hair dryer on wheels? I intended to remedy this error at once and acquire myself a Cannon Scooter.

I reached out to all of my 'contacts' (My contact Dave Spencer, who lives at 34 Devonshire Avenue, Leicester, asked me not to include his name in this book and I have honoured his wishes) and by the following morning I found this upon my doorstep...

The real life Cannon Scooter, the Vespa 150 TAP

The Vespa 150 TAP was invented by the French military in 1956. They took a humble 146 CC moped and made it awesome by attaching a M20 75 mm recoilless rifle (a U.S.-made light anti-armour cannon) to it. The cannon was actually embedded within the frame of the bike and the recoil was eliminated by venting gas out the rear of the weapon when it was fired.

The French weren't finished with the design yet, despite having invented the BEST. VEHICLE. EVER. They went one step further by having the Vespa parachuted behind enemy positions. Their name for this vehicle... the Bazooka Bike.

I was enthralled. I noted that attached to the bike, my contact (again I'm afraid I cannot identify the name of my contact. You see Dave Spencer, I've got your back), had left some sort of instruction book. I briefly flicked through the pages, something about using a tripod ... two-man team ... fire only when stationary ... then I remembered that I, Max Virtus, am a Captain of Bizarrchaeology, so I set fire to the instruction book at once, put the ashen remains in my catapult and launched them into the big blue.

It was time for a test drive. I leapt aboard the Bazooka Bike and I'm not afraid to admit that I let out a small squeal of joy as the engine came to life. Then I was off, roaring through the forests near my estate. The Vespa handled like a dream, the 75MM rifle proving rather light and manoeuvrable, allowing me to neatly avoid the many trees and rocks that attempted to block my path.

But I wasn't out here just for a test drive. Oh no, it was time to shoot that rifle. I spotted a large rock in the distance and, as I neared my target, I moved my hand to where the trigger would be, on the handle bars of the Vespa. Strangely there was nothing there, which would have struck me as odd, had I not noticed that the trigger was actually on the rifle itself. Hooking my feet around the handlebars I gingerly leaned backwards. In a hanging position, the heat of the engine gently buffeting my face, I reached out and was able to reach the rifle trigger. I pulled my head up, saw the rock was in range and then I pulled the trigger.

When I woke up two days later. I discovered that the Bazooka Bike had ended up being somersaulted into some overhead branches due to a combination of travelling speed, uneven terrain and firing a cannon whilst moving. I woozily got to my feet and noticed that the rock was untouched but a nearby tree had been explodified (it's a new word, I'm trying it out).

I later discovered that apparently you should never fire the cannon of a Bazooka Bike whilst riding it. Instead a two-man team would use a tripod to support and aim the cannon, whilst remaining completely stationary.

Which seems to me to be dreadfully dull.

Still, I now have added a Cannon Scooter to my warehouse. I thought my collection was complete, then I discovered that some brilliant brain had invented... a flying car. I decided to reach out to my contact (You see Dave Spencer three times I've mentioned my contact and still your identity remains completely secret) to see if he/she could procure such an item for me. I received disappointing news... flying cars do not exist. Sometimes a man has to do it himself (and do it himself in this case involves trying to figure out how to make a car fly).

How to make your car fly

When I sit in a traffic jam, trapped in an endless sea of gleaming metal monsters spreading out like a river towards the horizon, I find myself considering one thing in particular. Why can't my car fly?

It's a reasonable question. After all, my phone can share a tweet with a man in China, my watch can measure the number of calories I have so far burnt whilst sat in traffic (2 whole calories) and my sunglasses make me look very, very cool. So why can't my car gently arc up into the sky and glide majestically through the air?

Has anyone even bothered trying to invent a Flying Car? When I was a mini Max Virtus I certainly had an expectation that by 2016 my car would be able to fly (I also expected a hover-board, but let's not talk about how the unreasonable expectations set by Back to the Future 2, with its fantastical technology, ultimately broke my heart).

The answer is that someone did try to invent a flying car. And that someone was Raoul Hafner (helicopter pioneer and all around hero of Bizarrchaeology).

Back in 1942, Raoul decided to build a Jeep... that could fly. Which is not an easy thing to do. Military Jeeps weigh on average 2500 lbs, getting what is essentially a brick with wheels to leave the ground, without plummeting immediately back down to it, would take some doing.

Raoul's plan was deceptively simple, rather than going for the traditional approach of trying to invent a flying car by sticking wings to a regular auto-mobile, he instead opted to combine a helicopter with a Jeep. He took a rather dull Willys MB Jeep, then attached a 12.4 metre in diameter rotor to the top. The Willys was chosen as it could be dropped 8 feet in height without suffering any damage (not the same could be said for the poor soldiers sat inside it, they would have to pack some bean bags to absorb that buttock bruising experience) so once the rotors had deactivated and the Willys touched down at speed, it would be able to drive away (if your wheels fall off in the middle of a war zone that's just plain embarrassing).

Raoul then whacked some tail fairing and fins on the back of the Jeep so it could be steered whilst in the air and remain stable. He decided to call his invention... The RotaBuggy (the initial name Blitz Buggy, was probably dropped as it made it sound like some sort of insect spray).

The finished RotaBuggy in all its glory

Did it actually work? Would the Rotabuggy fly?

Initial tests went a little awry. The Rotabuggy was not able to pick up sufficient speed under its own engine to reach a suitable speed to lift off, nor could the lorry that tried to tow it on the next trial manage the feat.

This led to Raoul using a supercharged 4.5 litre Bentley automobile, and on the 27th of November 1943, it dragged the RotaBuggy up to speed before finally allowing the machine to become airborne and glide like a majestic winged brick at speeds of 45 mph. Improvements continued to be made and on February the 1st 1944, the Rotabuggy achieved a flight speed of 70 mph.

Raoul had done it. He had invented the flying car.

So why don't we drive (and fly) around in Gliding Cars today? Surely it would make that busy motorway much more palatable to simply float over it, taunting those who hadn't invested in a flying car down in the smog filled haze below.

Sadly, despite the awesomeness of the Rotabuggy, it was deemed irrelevant by the use of larger gliders that could carry a variety of vehicles, such as the anti-tank carrying Waco Hadrian or the Airspeed Horsa (a glider not a 5th century conqueror of southern Britain who was capable of flight.)

Which was a great shame, as if the development of the Rotabuggy had continued then maybe today we would have ... Flying Cars.

But don't curse the fickle gods of fate about the cruel lack of awesome flying cars for too long, it's time now to depart the Weapons and Armour collection, gather our horde of Hurscarls and go Vikinging.

Viking Treasure Horde

Whilst being set on fire, drifting on your longboat across the waves, proved a rather popular way of wrapping up your stay on Earth for many a Viking, it wasn't always the favoured choice. Sometimes it was best to be buried with all your possessions, what better way to ensure that you had everything you needed in Valhalla? Swords, armour, clothing, even food and wine would be found alongside the well prepared Viking in their tomb.

Now, it just so happens that several Viking tombs are located within my warehouse. Each cram packed with fascinating items of the past. Clearly they can't be removed. I don't want to be responsible for a Viking Hurscarl being without their favourite set of hair tweezers in the afterlife and looking like a hairy mess when they meet Odin. The All father is not fond of a monobrow. But that doesn't mean that I can't go rooting through this Treasure Horde and make some rather fascinating discoveries. You'll find out all about them in this sections escapades.

Those Weird Vikings

Vikings. Brilliant weren't they?

Stinky, blood thirsty, horned helmet wearing barbarians.

Only that sentence is depressingly untrue.

Firstly, Vikings were not stinky, in fact they were considered a fragrant bouquet of delight compared to their Saxon neighbours. Vikings bathed once a week and fashioned beauty products out of small animal bones, tweezers to pluck out unwanted hair and ear spoons to scoop out gunk from the lug holes of even the most fearsome warrior.

Secondly, Vikings weren't all that blood thirsty. In fact, their raiding hobby fast moved on to rather more boring interests, such as trading, settling and exploring (YAWN!).

Thirdly, there's no evidence to suggest that Vikings wore horns on their helmets. After all, why would anyone think it would be a good idea to stick two big easy to grab horns on the side of their head? It would allow a quick thinking opponent to either yank your head in position for a well-timed slash of a broadsword or simply pull your helmet over your eyes and provide chortlesome fun for all their friends as you stumble, blindly around the battlefield. In fact, there's very little evidence to suggest that Viking wore helmets AT ALL. Illustrations from the period show them wearing lousy leather caps or boringly bare headed.

So if Vikings aren't stinky, blood thirsty, horned helmet wearing barbarians then doesn't that make them rather boring? Oh no no dear reader, Vikings did plenty of bizarrely brilliant things.

Vikings loved Skiing

Who doesn't love Skiing? They answer is not Vikings. They loved it. Their skis were about 2 metres long and made of pine wood. However, Vikings didn't just ski, they also went ice skating. The skates were made from the foot bones of horses, cows or elks and were strapped to the feet of the Viking as they propelled themselves over the ice with two short sticks.

Are you thinking about a giant bearded Viking warrior involved in a pretty spectacular and surprisingly flexible ice skate dance routine whilst clad in horribly florescent and skin tight lycra? If not, you are now.

Wee Dye

Vikings considered the ideal hair colour to be blonde. They could also suffer from horrible infestations of lice and nits in their finely combed (yes, they had combs too) hair.

So what better solution than dunking your head in a month old bucket of wee?

Not only would it eliminate any rogue lice if would also lighten the colour of your hair.

However, having to keep month old buckets of wee could clutter up even the longest longhouse. So Lye Soap was developed instead. The key toxic ingredient of yee olde Lye Soap? Wee.

Vikings had a Weird Sense of Humour

Vikings took their reputations very seriously indeed. An insulted Viking would often respond to the verbal bashing by challenging the bully to a physical bashing instead. Duals would be held (not always resulting in death, sometimes the warrior who managed to disarm the other or draw first blood would be the victor) but what happened to the person who lost? Well, they were given a rather odd challenge. A wild cow would be brought into the hall where the duel had taken place. The cow's tail would then be shaved and coated in grease. Then the Viking who had lost the duel would have their feet covered in grease too. Then the cow would be made angry (calling it names or poking it in the eye with a stick should do the trick). Then the loser would have to grip the cow's tail (can you tell where this is going yet?).

On a given command the Viking would then have to pull the cow's tail. Which would make the cow go WILD! Bucking and stomping, kicking out with its hooves like a cowy whirlwind of death. The poor Viking would simply have to keep hold of its tail until it calmed down. If he succeeded, then not only could he keep his life he could also keep the cow as well! Bonus!

Secret Bonus Fact: Viking warriors wore eyeliner! It was called kohl and it was a dark coloured powder that kept the harsh light of the sun from damaging sensitive eyeballs.

How Thor is Marvel's Thor?

Thor. God of Thunder.

Thanks to a high ranking position in the pantheon of Viking gods and a commanding presence in the Marvel Cinematic Universe, Thor has continued to be one of the most well-known of all mythical deities.

Ask any one on Planet Earth to describe the God of Thunder and they will more than likely describe the recent Marvel incarnation, played by the actor Chris Hemsworth. In order to test this assumption, I conducted a survey (100,000 people were polled) and they described Thor as being good looking with long blond hair and possessing a muscular physique, super strength, ability to fly and a proud owner of a hammer.

But how close is the Marvel version of Thor to the original Viking incarnation? I, Max Virtus, have discovered just that, and the results are surprising!

Good Looks

Chris Hemsworth has blonde hair attached to a chiselled and clearly defined asymmetrical face. The real Thor did not. Instead he was considered to have fiery red hair and a bushy red beard (the Vikings considered beards a symbol of masculinity, so of course Thor would have the biggest, bushiest and beardiest beard possible). Marvel's Thor rocks a trendy and close cut face rug, yet the real Thor would have been more likely to possess a shaggy and scraggy crumb catcher.

But was he pretty (after all, one person I polled described Thor as 'hot as smouldering coals')?

That's not so clear cut, let's not forget that different cultures at varying times in their history considered a variety of physical attributes to be attractive. What I do know from reading the Poetic Eda is that the sight of Thor's face was so startling it scared Thrym the King of the Giants (admittedly Thor was dressed as a bride at the time, so that may have had something to do with it). His eyes weren't the striking blue of a Jedi lightsaber like Marvel's version either, instead they were bright red. The same King of the Giants described Thor's eyeballs as 'Why are Freyja's eyes so terrifying? They seem to be aglow with fire!' (Thrym called Thor 'Frejya' as Thor was disguised as the goddess Freyja at the time ... it's a long story, suffice to say Thor was wearing a lovely necklace of dangling housewives' keys and jewels on his chest and hair).

Ability to Fly

In the movies Thor flies around all over the place, this seems to be achieved by using his magical hammer Mjölnir like a ye olde jetpack. Could the mythical Thor achieve this same feat? The answer is no, Thor couldn't fly at all. However, his magic goats can (yes, you read that right, magic goats). Thor's goats were called Tanngrisnir and Tanngnjóstr and they would pull his magic chariot all over the place. And how does Thor repay these dutiful and loyal animal friends?

By eating them.

Every night Thor kills Tanngrisnir and Tanngnjóstr, chops them up and sticks them in a pot before noshing on stew À la goat. Then he reincarnates them the following morning so they can continue pulling his chariot. Which makes the evenings a pretty miserable time for Tanngrisnir and Tanngnjóstr. Worse was to come for those two loyal goats though when Thor and Loki (who weren't actually brothers, Thor had three brothers Baldr, Viðarr and Váli. Loki was still a concoction of frost giant and god and frequently shape shifted so full points for Marvel with that one) visited a small village and cooked up a goat hot pot for the peasants who lived there. Everyone had a lovely meal (apart from the goats of course) and when they had finished Thor instructed them to throw the goat's bones onto their skins so they can be reincarnated the next day. Morning rolls around and Thor resurrects his goats only to discover that one of them has a lame leg (one of those pesky peasants sucked the marrow out of a leg bone the night before). Thor is furious and is only placated when the villagers give Thor two of their children to work for him as servants. Thor accepts and then LEAVES HIS FRIENDLY, LOYAL AND MAGICAL GOATS BEHIND (when they need him the most!) in order to set back off home.

Those poor goats.

Magic Hammer

It's a big tick for Marvel as both Thors wield a magical hammer. However, whilst Marvel's Thor simply has the divine right to wave the hammer around (fulfilling the spell cast by Anthony 'Odin' Hopkins of 'Whosoever holds this hammer, if he be worthy, shall possess the power of Thor') the real Thor had to work a lot harder for it, needing to put on a pair of magical gloves and wear a strength enhancing belt to even be able to lift it. Other than that, the two weapons are virtually identical in power (Mjölnir means 'that which marks and pulverises to dust'). The two dwarves that forged the weapon describe it so;

'Then he gave the hammer to Thor, and said that Thor might smite as hard as he desired, whatsoever might be before him, and the hammer would not fail; and if he threw it at anything, it would never miss, and never fly so far as not to return to his hand.'

It's safe to say that Marvel's Thor and the Viking's Thor are different in several areas. But this provides a great opportunity for Marvel (Kevin Feige, I hope you're reading this). Just imagine if in the next Avengers film they made Thor an ugly, big bearded, red eyed, child stealing, goat eating, chariot riding god of thunder.

How bizarrely brilliant would that be? Because despite all of their differences, both Thors share one important similarity, they are both heroes.

The historian Merril Kaplan sums it up best;

"The mythological Thor is, of the Norse gods, the one closest to looking like a human hero, so if you were going to pull out a god from Norse mythology and make him into a hero working on behalf of mankind, Thor's your man. What I mean is that Thor in mythology is very much heroic in that he runs out and battles and saves people. He's the defender of the realm of gods and men. He goes out and smites trolls. He fights one-on-one. And in stories of human heroes, a lot of them are monster-slayers. So of all the Norse gods, Thor fits best with that idea of a hero.'

Dear Maxy,

IT'S YOUR MOTHER!

I wrote that in capitals just in case you happened to forget that I'm down in the dungeon, discovering the grossest, gruesomest, grim and grody historical facts I can find. Its unpleasant work let me tell you, I don't even have any of the facilities that a fine lady of my advanced years should expect... I had to have a rat gnaw off my toe nails the other day as I don't even have any nail clippers. No nail clippers. The inhumanity. It's just not right I tell you, it's just not right.

It's just that you never visit your old mother any more. If you did, then I wouldn't have had to tell you about my latest historical discovery through the medium of a letter. Goodness knows when a postman is ever going to visit me down here... especially when the last one had that unfortunate incident with the Iron Maiden and a Heretics Fork. We won't talk about that though. Not that the Postman can talk about it anymore. He had a lovely singing voice too.

Where was I? Oh YES. My discovery! Most people think that mummification was introduced by the Ancient Egyptians. You know, break the skull, pull out the brain, and stick the liver, stomach, intestines and lungs in a canopic jar and stuff what's left with Natron salt.

116

Simple. But I have discovered that those Egyptians were not the first to enjoy a spot of embalming. No, no, no.

You see, back in 6000BC the Chincorro people made some mummies too. The Chinchorro used to live in South America, around where Northern Chile and Southern Peru is today. Speaking of Southern Peru that's where I'm planning on taking my holidays this year Maxy. I hope you will take me. I've already prepared a bucket of suntan lotion and an extraordinarily wide brimmed hat in anticipation.

Anyways, I thought I would tell you about how the Chinchorro used to mummify people... and because I love cooking (who can have forgot my thick crusted eel pie?) I decided I would share the information in the style of a recipe book. You can put it next to your one pot crocodile cook book I got you last Christmas. I do spoil you Maxy.

Chinchorro Mummy

Ingredients:

1 Dead Body

3 Stones

2 Buckets of Tar

4 Sharp Sticks

8 Lumps of Coal

A Pile of Ash

• First of all, you need a dead body. Do check that the body is dead before turning them into a mummy as they may well be cross if they are just sleeping. The best way to check on how dead a person is, I find, is to be polite and just ask them if they are dead.

• Find yourself a large sharp stone. There should be plenty about, it is the Stone Age after all. What sort of Stone Age would a Stone Age be if it didn't have any Stones in it?

• Use the large sharp stone to cut the legs, arms and head off the torso. This is surprisingly tricky so you might want to bring a friend along to help you out. It's good to share, remember?

• Then very carefully you take a small sharp stone (how will you know it's a small sharp stone? It will be smaller than the large sharp stone, that's how!) And slice off all the skin on the torso. Make sure you keep the skin to one side as you will need it later. You need to take the skin off the arms and legs too, make it easier for yourself by rolling it off the limbs like a saggy pair of tights.

•   Then cut into the torso and remove all the organs, you don't need to keep them though! Just ensure you dispose of them safely and hygienically, by feeding them to your dog or something.

•   Fill the vacant torso with hot coals to dry it out, just be careful you don't set the thing on fire! You'll be bleaching that smell out your nostrils for months.

•   Now, go back to the arms and limbs, plunge into them with your sharp stone and remove all the bones. You don't need these either, so throw them away. Just make sure they're not curved as they have a habit of returning to you.

•   Replace the bones with a stick, imagine a giant cocktail stick, and then spike them back onto the body. Don't be zany and try mixing up where arms and legs should be, just stick them back where they originally came from.

•   Once your body is all back in one piece you can fill the torso with cool ash and grass so it resembles a body shape again. Do them a favour, give them a six pack or bulging biceps whist you're packing it.

•   Then all you have to do is cover the body in paste made from white ash, it's a bit like glue so you can use this to stick the head back on too.

- Put the skin back on the body, this is tricky and time consuming! Best way to do it is by imagining you're putting pyjamas on. But instead of pyjamas it's skin.

- Then cover the body with black tar, let it dry and... TA - DAH! You're finished!

So why did the Chinchorro people go to all this trouble? Well, it's quite simple, this process has allowed you to turn a loved family member into a giant doll. Now you can bring it with you wherever you go! The Chinchorro used to do just that, posing the body and then bringing it along to important celebrations. That way you could have all your family there with you. Sounds lovely doesn't it?

Well Maxy that's all from me for today, I've got to get back to it. Do pop down and see me sometime though. I'll prepare a lovely casserole. Not that I have much in the way of food down here but I do have a surprising number of cobwebs, dust and rat droppings. It'll be a lovely casserole indeed.

Big hugs, love and kisses.

Your Mum

The Agōgē

There are many great words.

Philtrum (the bits just between the middle of your lips and the bottom of your nose and where despite intense meditation and regular shaving I am still unable to grow any facial hair).

Kazoo (I love this word, it's the only name for a muscial instrument that sounds like a comic book sound effect. I can just see Batman elbow dropping a thug with an explosion called Kazoo emanating from his armpit).

Beige (so … many … vowels)

And Agōgē. Just trying saying it, it's a delight of tongue wiggling and lip wavering.

The Agōgē is training. For the Spartans of Ancient Greece, it was an intense trial to transform its population into warriors capable of being the 'Walls of Sparta' (Sparta had no physical walls on instruction of the city's mythical founder Lycurgus. Who either wanted to ensure that his people were fighting fit to defend what was theirs or he just wanted to avoid suffering from Wallophobia*) for you it will allow you to experience how best to become a Soldier or Hero of Ancient Greece. So push out those press-ups cover yourself with baby oil and turn the page (just make sure you wash your hands first).

*Possibly not a real phobia. But with Xanthophobia (the fear of the colour yellow), Pogonophobia (the fear of beards) and Omphalophobia (fear of the human navel) all being real perhaps there is a good chance it could be. Incidentally, surely Omphalophobia leads to Spectrophobia (a fear of mirrors) and Acrophobia (a fear of looking down) just in case they spot their own belly button winking back at them? Answers to the back of a postcard displaying a photo of a bare midriff to Virtus Castle please.

7 (Painful) steps to gaining the Physique of a Hoplite

Every morning when I awake, wrapped within the plush duvet laid upon my Hästens Vividus bed, I steel my nerves and ready myself. Why? Because in precisely 26 minutes and 54 seconds my morning workout session will begin. Starting with a 20 mile run (backwards of course, otherwise where is the challenge?), I then move on to do 400 push-ups, 300 sit ups, 500 lunges and 250 Bulgarian split squats (the answer is, yes, they are as painful as they sound).

Yet even my brutal training regime pales in comparison to that of the Spartans, those delightful war loving Ancient Greeks of ye olden days (the official term for anything that happened before right now).

The Spartans made sure that every single citizen of Sparta was a Hoplite solder and to become a Spartan Hoplite and therefore be allowed to be a citizen you had to undergo...

The Agōgē

(Before you read that title make sure you add the Sound Effect of DUH DUH DUUUUUUUUUUUUH! to ensure the suitable level of drama is achieved).

At the moment there's a lot of workout regimes that profess to the exercise fanatic that they will allow you to achieve Spartan levels of fitness. It is safe to say that a real Spartan would look briefly at these exercises before punching them in the face, pulling their hair and calling them rude names.

If you want to be a REAL Spartan Hoplite, then all you have to do is follow this simple seven step program;

(Please note that the author, Max Virtus, accepts no responsibility for any accidental fatal injury that should occur if someone were to actually try the seven step programme).

STEP 1

So when should your Spartan training begin? Well, if you are reading this then chances are you are already too old to begin your Spartan training (unless of course you are a terrifyingly advanced new born baby that has developed the ability to read) because your Agōgē would commence as soon as you were born. An Elder would come and inspect a baby to check if it was fit and healthy enough to live. If not? The child would be left in the wilderness near Mount Taygetus to die from the elements (or if the child did survive the next few days it might be brought back to Sparta to continue its training).

STEP 2

You passed the first step? Then it's on to step two. At the age of 7 you would be taken away from your family and your REAL training would begin and would last for the next 22 years. Only once you reached the age of thirty would your Agōgē be complete and you would be allowed to do boring normal things like marry someone or have children.

STEP 3

In the early days of your training you would have to steal to eat. On the plus side you would only be punished if you were caught. On the negative side that punishment involved being beaten by a big stick. A lot.

How to recreate this in the modern day? Only eat one apple a day. And nothing else.

The Spartans liked to ensure that they looked suitably ripped, so not eating certainly helped reduce their body fat (it also meant that their armies needed remarkably little food in the field, after all, an army marches on its stomach ... and its feet too but that's beside the point). I couldn't imagine eating this little, after all I can't leave hunger locked up till lunch without a bowl of my Captain Virtus Crunch (available in all good supermarkets).

STEP 4

You would only be given one item of clothing a year to wear (items of clothing like a red cloak called a Phoinikis, not a comedy pair of glasses or a wimple). If you lost this item or it was torn, too bad. No Lycra shorts, training vests and expensive trainers for a real Spartan.

STEP 5

With Step 5 things started to get a bit more serious (steps 1 - 4 should have been pretty easy) as you would be enrolled as part of the Spartan Secret Police and then sent off to kill some slaves who were looking shifty and rebellious. After all, those pesky Helots have to be kept in line, who else will peel you a grape when you become a citizen? You could kill any slaves who were out at night who you witnessed speaking seditiously with each other, which in the modern day would mean you would have to try and kill EVERYONE (please note don't actually try this at home).

STEP 6

Make sure you keep an eye on your waistline during your training, put on a few pounds and you risk being publicly ridiculed and humiliated by your chums. Continue to pile on the poundage and you would be exiled from Sparta and also nicknamed the 'Chubinator' (Please note; only one of these two statements are true).

STEP 7

You finished your training! Hurrah! Or at least you had better hope you are able to complete your training. If you haven't then you don't get to be a citizen which leaves you one option, to become a slave.

The next thing to consider is not to embarrass yourself in battle, this involves not running away screaming like a petrified squirrel when you face a Persian advance as well as making sure you arrive in time for the fight. According to ancient historian with a beard, Herodotus, two Spartans who arrived late (I think the reason they gave was something about being stuck behind a slow moving horse) and missed the famous battle of Thermopylae were so ashamed and humiliated that one of them killed himself, the other ultimately gained forgiveness by dying gloriously in a later battle.

In battle as a Spartan your options were pretty limited, win or die. Running away to fight another day wasn't a choice. That's why a mother would say to her son before a battle "Return with your shield or on it" (which is a bit different to "don't forget to buy some milk, clean behind your neck and tie up your shoelaces").

So forget Men's Health magazine, forget celebrity endorsed fitness DVDs, all you need to do is follow the Simple Seven Step program to be a Spartan Hoplite and one day you too could look like a pumped up baby oiled buffed up delight for the eyeballs (just don't refer to yourself in that way), marching forward in slow motion looking mean and moody which is an impressive feat whilst wearing only a pair of pants and a crimson cape like a real Spartan should (although, that would be ridiculous, you may be a Spartan but you are definitely still going to wear some armour. And as for a cape? Never wear a cape in battle it's only going to get snagged on something and trip you up in an embarrassing fashion*).

*Sorry Batman.

In fact, 9 out of 10 Spartans agree that its best to wear armour and avoid dying when shot at with an arrow.

How not to die when shot at with an Arrow

As I, Max Virtus, (Captain of Adventure and Expert of Bizarrchaeology – I know you know that but I just like to reaffirm it, you might have lost this book briefly in a confusing adventure with a hungry seagull and a warrior monk and only just recovered it*) sit here in my mahogany furnished office (floor, walls, desk, chair, light, lampshade, coffee cup and pipe... all gleaming mahogany) I find myself contemplating the humble arrow. Not the most exciting of items in my warehouse of odd history but without a doubt a hugely influential one (although equal credit must go to the humble bow, without it, the humble arrow would be absolutely rubbish).

Ever since the bow and arrow was invented, approximately 10,000 BC (no one knows the exact date but I believe it to be 10,001, four months, two weeks, three days, four hours, twenty-two minutes and thirty-five seconds BC*2) it radically altered the life of the caveman. No longer did the hunter have to frantically dash after a Woolly Mammoth, waving their spear haphazardly in the air. Instead they could launch arrows from a safe distance to their hearts content, until the mighty beast was reduced to dinner.

Which was brilliant for the caveman. The problem came about (and the reason for my musing) when people decided to shoot other people with their arrows. This of course hurt... a lot (I know this to be a fact having shot arrows at my bizarrchaeology intern, Ian. He said that it hurt a lot and who am I to doubt him?)

Initially the great minds of the Ancient world determined that the best way not to die when shot by an arrow was to avoid being shot by an arrow in the first place. The problem with this came about when some pesky general was paying you to attack an enemy force and that involved them shooting lots and lots of arrows at you. Shields were good, obviously, at stopping these arrows from jabbing into delicate flesh. The formidable Hoplon shield of the Greek Hoplite, as well as the close knit, shoulder to shoulder Phalanx formation, proved particularly effective in the criteria of not dying when shot at with an arrow. But this wasn't enough for the Hoplites, they needed further protection... enter the Linothorax, the most effective armour in the Ancient Greek world!

What was this armour like in order to be so potent? Hardened iron dipped in concrete and coated in ninjas? No. It was made from Linen.

So what is the Linothorax? Quite simply a breast plate made of many layers of linen glued together with animal fat.

Would you wear something made of a summer holiday material and be shot at with an arrow at point blank range. No? Well, I, Captain Max Virtus, was prepared to do that. It is my mission as a Captain of Bizarrchaeology to face danger in the pursuit of history. I just needed someone to shoot an arrow at me in order to test how effective the armour was. Fortunately, Ian, my intern, was available to do just that. (He wasn't that keen on the idea due to fear of causing me premature death, once I assured him that the only thing I fear is an emu he was suitably reassured. Although he didn't have much choice in the matter, despite his protesting it was clearly written in his contract that if or when I needed to be shot with a bow and arrow, crossbow, shruiken, cannon, trebuchet or laser he would be the man for the job).

So, I donned the Linothorax from my collection, and then went off to find a bow and arrow. In order to ensure historical accuracy, I opted for a Persian short bow. I then stood ten feet away from Ian, and instructed him to aim the bow and draw the string. Ian mentioned something about 'risk assessments', I didn't catch the rest as he had accidentally released the string and shot me.

Was I injured? Well ultimately yes... but that was due to Ian missing my chest entirely and accidentally shooting me in the leg. After several attempts, Ian finally managed to shoot me in the chest (not to mention the elbow, left ear lobe and big toe. I can now report that being shot point blank range with an arrow was absolutely fine (as long as it's in the chest). In fact, the arrow barely penetrated the Linothorax.

So there you have it, conclusive proof. How not to die when shot at with an arrow according to the Ancient Greeks? Wear a Linothorax. Just make sure you only get shot in the chest.

* I'm pretty sure that was the weirdest segway yet.
*2 I have absolutely no historical evidence to back up this statement.

How to Be a Mythical Hero

Now you're Spartan fit and equipped with Armour its time to take your final step in the Agōgē, to become a Mythical Hero.

Ever since Heracles first adorned his head with the mane of the Nemean Lion and realised that he looked both stylish, sophisticated and manly, everyone has wanted to be a Hero. In the moden day that love for the (Super)Hero has gone worldwide, with every other film released based on a comic hero who orginated in glorious technicolour on the printed page. Yet the links between Super Hero and Mythical Hero are clear. Despite the interverning two thousand-ish years there recently isn't that much difference between them.

Iron Man is a hero because he has loads and loads of money and technology to have the best weapons and armour, yet his main weakness is his pride and arrogance in his own abilities and intelligence. Agamemnon was considered a hero of the trojan war because he had loads and loads of money and technology to ensure that he had the best weapons and armour for his army, yet his weakness and undoing was his hubris (I initially thought hubris was some kind of pate but it's actually excessive pride)... and the fact that he killed his own daugher to get wind (not gaseous wind, that would be weird, wind to blow his ships to Troy).

Superman is unstoppable apart from his one weakness that EVERYONE knows about, an extreme allergy to Kryptonite. Archilles was unstoppable apart from his one weakness that EVERYONE knew about, his Archilles' heel (seriously? If you don't want everyone to know about the one weak point upon your body you should call it something else. Like Geoff's heel (or Terry's heel, he's already got an orange, why not a heel too?), don't use your own name, that's just asking to be shot by an arrow).

Spiderman is a hero because he has magical Spider juice in his veins. Heracles was a hero because he had magical Zeus juice in his veins (that sounded weirder that I was expecting).

So, there are a plethorate (I love my dictionary) of links between heroes of the modern world and the Ancient world. This means that we could have a hero of the ancient world being heroic in the modern world. Why not? All they need is the right guidance, a series of top tips to ensure that they know how to Hero with the best and the rest of them..

Who would be their teacher? Max Virtus of course. I have the agoge for training, I have the top tips, all I need is the student... and that could be you dear reader! So grab your Xiphos and get ready, as I transform you into a Mythical Hero.

Don't learn how to Sword Fight

Despite the entertainment industry's best attempts to convince me, the most effective way to defeat your opponent in a duel to the death is NOT by ensuring you always hit your swords together. The actual intention is to miss the opponent's sword entirely and hit their body. Therefore as a mythical hero you should cut the following supposedly heroic moves from your repertoire.

Spinning

No Spinning. The Star Wars prequels may well have taught a legion of would be Jedi Knights that the best way to do battle is by furiously twisting like an alocholic with a bottle of wine and a blunt corkscrew, but repeatedly exposing your back to your opponent and losing sight of what they're doing is not the best idea for a Mythical Hero to stay alive.

Rolling

Why are you rolling around on the floor? Stop it. That includes backward rolls. It looks cool in film but that's because they have plenty of attempts to get it right. Chances are that if you try that in a real sword fight that you'll only impale yourself on your own blade or accidentally slice open a major artery. Either way this will result in awkard embarrassment and premature death.

Back Flips

That's the equivalent of a spin whilst rolling and is frowned upon in the Sword Fighting community.

Swinging on Ropes

Desipte the temptation, avoid swinging on a conveniently positioned rope in a sword fight (this includes chandeliers) it's rather tricky holding on to your sword whilst doing so and unlike most actors you don't have a wire work team to keep you suspended in mid air. Also, don't do a pirate and hold your sword in your teeth, that results in sliced lips and a permenent smile.

Don't Parry

Were you not listening before? Stop hitting your opponnent's sword.

That was all pretty negative, if a Mythical Hero can't do any of that stuff in a sword fight, what can they do? Well, they should take a leaf from a Greek Hoplite's book and simply use the jab.

That's all you need to sword fight like a Mythical Hero. The Jab. Simply extend your sword arm at rapid pace and embed it in your enemy's flesh before they do the same to you. Your Xiphos sword is short (eighteen inches give or take) but it is ideally suited to be positioned behind your shield to be poked out from around the side to surprise your foe. Bring the pointy bit of the blade flashing out over the top, left, right, or bottom of the shield, keep your enemy guessing at to where your next attack is coming from. Incidentally that's why you don't need to parry, you have a nice round Hoplon Shield to hide behind (made of hefty wood with a bronze coating, the Hoplon or Aspis is going to keep your delicate and frail human body protected by covering up your shoulder all the way down to your thigh) you can even use the handle positioned at the rim to ram the sheild into an unsuspecting warrior.

Your shield also proves handy at slamming down on an enemy's toes. Regardless of how much armour resides on your opponent's body their feet fingers will still be poking out of their sandals. What better way to greet them by slamming your shield down upon them? Sure to open up the defences of even the most sturdy of opponents.

In conclusion, to swordfight like a hero just practise the jab, each and every day and victory will be yours.

Have a Dark Origin story

Any superhero worth their salt has an origin forged in despair and suffering. Batman's parents were murdered in front of him, Superman's entire home planet was destroyed and Spiderman couldn't save his Uncle's life. To be a mythical hero though you have to go eighteen steps further. Your origin story has to be **<u>DARK</u>** (underlined, bold and in capitals to suggest how dark that origin story is).

Let's look at the Hero of all Heroes; Heracles (or Hercules if you're Roman). Disney teach children that Heracles had to prove himself worthy to live on Mount Olympus with his father, Zeus, by completing 12 labours, that's because the real reason was not family friendly.

Heracles killed his entire family. The 12 labours (originally 10 but that pesky King Eurystheus kept changing the rules) were an opportunity for Heracles to seek redemption. It's the equivelent of Bruce Wayne being the one who shot his parents rather than a faceless gangster.

Learn Pankration

All superheroes have their own fighting style, something distinctive that let's the unfortunate villain know who's pummeling him, just from the angle of the punch against his face. But all fighting styles pale againt Pankration. And that is the fighting style you're going to need to learn if you're going to be a mythical hero. It was either Thesesus or Heracles who developed Pankration and the fact that it allows you to defeat Minotaurs, Nemean Lions and Cerberus means it is highly effective. It works so well by pretty much throwing everything at your enemy, even the kitchen sink (especially the kitchen sink, those taps can sting).

Virtually anything goes with Pankration, there's only three things you can't do. Bite your enemy, pluck out their eyeballs or damage their genitals. Other than that feel free to strangle, punch, kick and throw to your heart's content.

That's more than enough to get any would be modern mythical heroes started. With a combination of a dark and disturbing backstory, sword skills and fighting ability you should be well on your way to defeating heinous and fiendish monsters before ultimately dying in a tragic way (usually dying alone. Take Bellerophon. He was a hero who had defeated the chimera. He had a flying horse, he was the king and was happily married with four children. Yet he managed to mess that all up by trying to visit Zeus, who sent a gadfy to attack him, resulting in Bellerophon crashing to the ground and ending up crippled and alone for offending the gods).

The Pirate Frigate

A few weeks ago my attempts to create a Megalodon (What can I say? I'd just watched Jurrassic World whilst eating far too many gummy bears. The resulting sugar fuelled hallucinations led to this slightly misconveived plan) were met with limited success, strands of DNA everywhere (it's a pain to get out of carpets) and a very large and very empty swimming pool. I needed to fill this enormous span of water with something – it made perfect sense for that something to be a Pirate Frigate!

The only people who don't love Pirates are those who watched Cutt Throat Island (just say no to Cutt Throat Island kids) for everyone else get ready to dive in to a sea of discovery as I reveal what I learnt aboard my ship.

Who wouldn't want to be a Golden Age Pirate?

My Great, great, great, great, great grandfather was a Pirate. Shocking fact, I know (although not as shocking as what my great, great, great grandfather did for a living, but that's an escapade for another day). His name? Captain Quintus Virtus. I read through his journal the other day (I found it secreted in a dust coated treasure chest within the alligator compound) and within it he recounted how he loved nothing better than to stand atop his Bowsprit (that's the pointy bit at the front of his flagship, the 300-ton vessel; 'The Vengeance of Virtus'.

Unlike myself my Great, great, great, great, great grandfather was a massive egomaniac and enjoyed naming the objects after himself), the sea breeze fluttering through his golden locks, his bulbous nose being stung by the salty depths below and he would bellow out in joyful song;

'Yo Ho! Yo Ho! A Pirate's Life for Bee!'

Now clearly this never quite caught on. However, Quintus had a point, back in 1710AD, during the Golden Age of Piracy there was more than likely to better life than that of a Pirate. Being a regular sailor usually meant being blackjacked over the head in your favourite pub to awake the next day in the Navy with only a salt biscuit to keep you company. From that point onwards you had a 50/50 chance of either managing to get back home (and probably never being paid for your hard labour) or contracting a rather unhealthy bout of gout.

Instead a Pirate chose their life, received an equal share of any booty, got to vote on who should be the next Captain and also on important ship decisions, had their own island paradise to hang out at (the beautiful New Providence Island in the Bahamas) and also (if modern films would have us believe) be the only people in existence who could make wearing leather pantaloons look cool.

So why did Qunitus decide to be a Pirate? What were his main reasons? I have found out dear reader and now you can too!

Reason 1. You can grow amazing facial hair and then set it on fire

This Pirate's beard is particularly impressive as he's trimmed it in the shape of a giant rectangle

Yes, reason one is that being a Pirate sets you free from any strict requirements of society to keep your facial hair moderate and unassuming. Now clearly the facial hair of a Beard World Championship competitor (Yes. The Beard World Championship is a real competition) wouldn't be appropriate for climbing rigging (there would always be the risk that a fellow pirate would mistake your beard for rigging and try to climb that instead, disappear up your nose and never be seen again) you can still have fantastic facial hair. Take the infamous Pirate Edward 'Blackbeard' Teach who used to set his beard on fire using slow burning fuses stuffed into his beard and hair. The effect of this technique would be to give off a heavy, greasy smoke that would surround Blackbeard, making him look like a devil emerging from the gates of hell (although the smog emerging from his face must have made Blackbeard an unpopular guest at a dinner party). Blackbeard even went so far as to shape his beard to resemble the form of a Kraken, a fearsome and mythical sea beastie from the deep dark blue.

Reason 2: The Jolly Roger didn't look like a Jolly Roger

Now the Jolly Roger wasn't just one design (the classic but slightly dull skull and crossbones over a black background) instead it could be just about anything. A Pirate Captain would go absolutely wild and unleash all their creativity and love for sticky black plastic and colour coordination in order to create the best Pirate flag ever. Something that combined both a fear factor with a certain artistic integrity.

Take the flag of the Pirate Christopher Moody for example. He went with a striking red background in order to really capture the attention of his audience (that would be the sobbing Merchant crew on the nearby galleon) and combined it with an elegant yellow winged hourglass to suggest to his enemies that there time was running out (well 'flying' out I suppose), in the centre of the image was a big arm clutching a dagger to symbolise the fact that Christopher was very proud of his arm definition from all those jumping press ups (or the fact that his ship and crew were very, very powerful... you decide). The yellow skull and crossbones suggests that whilst Christopher was still a traditionalist he liked to appear to be a bit zany too.

Reason 3: Pirates don't bury treasure

Perhaps this isn't that exciting a reason, apart from when you consider that books, films, TV, video games, comics and Johnny Depp would have us believe that Pirates suffered from some strange compulsion to bury all of their treasure on a remote and highly inaccessible island rather than, well, spend it. Quintus' journal reliably informed me that this simply didn't happen. Most pirate treasure consisted of tasty vittles (that's a fun word), silks and other valuable items like tobacco, gunpowder and sugar. Things that if you were to bury in a large ditch would end up with more mould on them than the stick of long forgotten celery in the back of my salad tray (I only rediscovered it during an unexpectedly terrifying trip to the fridge for a midnight snack. I'm pretty sure the celery in question had grown so gungey that it had led to the creation of new life).

Pirates didn't need a complex map with a large X to mark the spot in order to find their treasure as they had already spent it (only one Pirate ever buried their treasure, Captain William Kidd. That was an attempt to have some sway over the authorities who were hot in pursuit, sadly it didn't work as he was still hung for being all piratey).

A Pirate's Life for Me

There you have it, the reasons why Captain Quintus Virtus decided to become a Pirate. And I think we can all agree that they are compelling indeed. After all, who wouldn't want to be an elaborate beard growing flag embroidering treasure spending man (or woman, Pirates were leagues ahead with gender equality compared to the rest of the world).

We now interrupt this book with a random thought

Here in my Warehouse of Bizarrchaeology I regularly receive letters saying 'Hey Max, I believe that the world is falling apart. That things are the worst that they have ever been or could ever be.' They then list the reasons why things are so much worse than they have ever been in the history of forever. I've compiled all their reasons and it's an absolute check list of horror. A check list that grows ever more horrifying the further you read.

- Violence
- Plague
- War
- Hunger
- One Direction

But the simple fact is, that throughout history, people have always thought that things are at their worst. Chances are that isn't the case. Unless they said it whilst living in the 17th century, in which case they would have been absolutely right... the world was falling part.

How come I hear you ask? It was all to do with 'The Little Ice Age' (which wasn't an animated film starring a lovable quartet of furry prehistoric animals on a quest for a new home whilst going through a series of entertaining and ultimately life affirming adventures, instead it was a far more boring climate change dating from the 14th to the 19th centuries) which at its peak made things rather chilly for people in the 17th century. Brainiacs are divided on why things got so tepid but it was either something to do with sunspots (or a lack of them, which led to less radiation from the sun and so causing a lack of sandal weather) or volcanoes (12 volcanoes went Kablooey* during the 17th century leading to increased dust veils in the sky which could have caused a sun blockage, a bit like coating the Earth in a giant bottle of Protect and Bronze Nivea sun cream).

So the weather got a bit nippy, why would that make the 17th century the worst ever period of history to live in? The first thing to consider is that weather and climate are two very different things; when the weather gets cold you put on a jumper, when the climate gets cold you turn into an ice-cube. A colder climate leads to less food, which leads to hungry people, that leads to grumpy people, which leads to angry people, which leads to lots of wars. Don't believe me? Here's the proof.

In the 17th century you had...

- The English Revolution (or the Civil War. Not that historians call it the Civil War, it was actually one of the Wars of Three Kingdoms just to be extra confusing).
- The Collapse of the Ming Dynasty in China (cold climate meant less rice which resulted in the death of 30% of the people in the country).
- The Russian Famine that saw off a third of their total population.

- The Gunpowder Plot.
- Worker uprisings in Italy.
- The Moghul Wars of Succession.
- The 30 Years War (unlike the 100 Years War the 30 Years War actually lasted for 30 Years. The war was so devastating across various regions that disease and famine caused massive population losses over Italy and Germany as well as some financial bankruptcy for the countries involved).
- The Mauritanian Thirty Years' War (different to the other 30-year war, this one took place in Mauritania and the Western Sahara. However, it still lasted thirty years. So 100% accuracy on its name).
- The Great Turkish War (Not that great for the Ottoman Empire, they lost a bunch of countries by the end of it)

In fact, over 100 years there were 90 different wars with a total battle time of 428 years (wars took a lot longer to fight, primarily because there was a lot more walking involved). Add to this the drop in temperature of one degree, which led to the Baltic Sea being frozen over and most rivers in Europe freezing. This meant an extended winter, reducing the growing seasons and this lead to widespread crop failure and famine, which resulted in a hefty population decline. People couldn't even fish because all the cod had migrated south to warmer waters.

So the next time someone tells you that 'Things aren't like they were in the good old days'. Just be very, very, very, very, very, very grateful.

*This is a real word used by volcanologist. Honest.

Pirate FAQ

So, you took the advice of my great, great, great, great, great grandfather Captain Quintus Virtus and decided that a Pirate's Life really was for you. And who can blame you? After all, who wouldn't want to wear a pair of knee high leather boots, a striped shirt with floppy sleeves and have a parrot strapped on their shoulder? First of all, don't do any of those things. You'll be keel hauled by your crew before you can say 'Arggghh Jim Lad, polly want a cracker who be shivering my timbers with a piece of eight?!'

So what should you do? How should you behave? What should you wear? These are all reasonable questions for any novice golden age pirate to ask before their first voyage. That's why I've assembled this list of Frequently Asked Questions (and the answers too, otherwise it would be terribly unhelpful) so that the pirate novice can have their mind put at ease. So let's start with the most frequently asked question...

Can I wear makeup?

That Johnny Depp sure has a lot to answer for (the first of them being, Johnny... why have you stopped being in good films?! Mortedai?! Transcendance?! The Lone Ranger?! Why do you hurt me Johnny? Why?! Do you do it on purpose? To so casually discard my feelings?! Why Johnny? Wh – I just might have got a little carried away there) the second is Jack Sparrow.

After all the tottering, moustachioed, make up wearing marauder is surely not an accurate representation of a genuine corsair? More accurate than you would think. Wearing mascara would be a sensible course of action for a pirate. After all, it worked for the Vikings (what? The Vikings weren't pirates? Wash your mouth out with lye soap. 'Viking' or 'Vikinger' literally means 'to pirate'. So Viking is a verb and a noun. Or a Voun. Or a Nerb.) Who would slap on some kohl under their eyes. The black ore and lead material of Kohl would absorb the harsh rays of the sun bouncing off the sea or reflecting from the helmet of a nearby Saxon knight and so help prevent the Viking from taking their eye off the battle. So, some Vikings wore Kohl, and Vikings are pirates which means pirates wore makeup. You can't dispute that.

Are earrings acceptable ear wear?

Of course. In fact it would be considered a bit weird if as a pirate you didn't have earrings. It was a well-known fact amongst Pirate crews that having your ears pierced with valuable and expensive metals like gold and silver improved your eyesight. Which is why the famous portrait of William Kidd by Howard Pyle clearly shows the captain wearing an earring.

Admittedly its near impossible to see Kidd's earing in this painting. It's there though, twinkling right at you

Whilst the pirates viewed the combination of ritual and expensive metals being responsible for a level up in vision clarity, it had more to do with the area in which the ear was pierced. In a weird way, uneducated and rather smelly sailors proved to be forerunners of medical science. Modern acupuncturists now pierce certain areas of the ear (along with the face and feet) to treat conditions like near sightedness and conjunctivitis.

Can I have an Eye Patch, Peg Leg or a Hook for a Hand?

Famous literary pirates like Captain Hook and Long John Silver are famous for their fake appendages but what about real pirates? Would you be laughed off your frigate if you rocked up with a missing extremity replaced by a bit or wood or metal? The answer is... kind of.

Clearly the chance of losing a limb as a pirate was a definite possibility. Not just from the dangers of battle and the chance of an over eager naval officer attempting to lop off a ligament with cannon or cutlass but also from the accidental dangers you could find aboard your own ship (after all, most accidents occur at home) in the form of some loose rigging or a dropped anchor.

This constant danger led to one of the very first forms of health insurance. In fact, the Pirate Captain Henry Morgan drew up an incredibly comprehensive list of compensations should a pirate be injured in an upcoming assault on Panama. Anybody in his 2,000-strong pirate crew was entitled to 600 pieces of eight for the loss of a hand or a foot, 1,800 pieces for the loss of both legs, 200 pieces for one eye, and 2,000 pieces for total blindness -- that's approximately £300,000 in modern currency. This generous pay-out suggests that after the injury a pirate would not be able to supplement his income with any future raiding. Which would be about right, whilst the technology existed to replace a missing limb with a hook or peg it would have made life extremely treacherous aboard a frigate upon stormy waters or in a protracted bout of Navy warfare. The final pay out was aptly named, more often than not it was your final pay out.

Wait, you didn't really answer my question?

No, I didn't but I answered that one. Next.

Can a woman be a Pirate?

There's been a long held belief by many a sailor, that allowing a woman aboard a ship is bad luck. But that didn't bother pirates, because if the woman is a fierce, strong and powerful sailor then it's surely much luckier to have her aboard then to leave her at home? Considering the era that the golden age of piracy occurred within, and the general rights, equality and benefits that women had in society (answer; they didn't) pirate crews were incredibly progressive. Chin Shih (whilst making her appearance in the 1800s, long after the peak of Golden

Age piracy in 1700 to 1730AD) was probably the most successful and wealthiest pirate of all time, she had control over a fleet of 1500 ships and some 60'000 pirates. That's a whole lot of pirates. Over her pirating career Chin Shih did it all, making a vast fortune and even defeating the Chinese Navy in battle before finally retiring and living off her wealth till the ripe old age of 69 (and considering most pirates ended up being hanged long before their 69th birthday this is particularly impressive).

Will I ever fight a Ninja?

Ninjas VS Pirates? Now that's my kind of question. Is there any historical evidence for this? No. But if your heart is true and your dreams are pure then wondrous things can happen! In fact, because my admin Ian really hasn't had a lot to do since the incident with the arrow and the linothorax, I had him run a highly complex and very scientific virtual reality simulation through the Virtus computer to see who would win between Pirate and Ninja. The answer was surprising, they wouldn't fight instead they would team up and create an unstoppable, extremely stealth and water loving warrior called a Pinja. Fact. *

*Not a Fact.

The Ultimate Challenge

Congratulations. You've done very well at the dual task of reading and turning pages. Now we reach the point of yours and mine Ultimate Challenge. Wait, wait, wait, that font really doesn't get across how Ultimate this Ultimate Challenge is. Let's try this instead;

THE

ULTIMATE

CHALLENGE

That did it.

So what is the Ultimate Challenge?

I asked my intern Ian (yep, that guy again, he's like a rash. Not because he's irritating but because he covers himself from head to toe in sudocream. It's a weird habbit) to create me a challenge that would require all of the knowledge I'd gained through writing this journal in order to survive. That's right, the consequences of failing in this activity would be fatal.

I left Ian to work on this task for 13 weeks, 13 days, 13 minutes and 13 seconds. He constructed the trap on the 13th floor of apartment 13, within the large building on 13th street.

After having eaten a filling final meal of 13 courses, I set off to complete the challenge at 13:00 on Friday the 13th. I hadn't slept that well the night before as a dog was howling outside my castle, which meant my mum, who was feeling a bit sick, kept on shouting at the dog to be quiet. She must have been banging an object against her floor three times to try and scare the dog off, I wasn't sure what the object was as it was a most peculiar noise.

Anyway, as I took my brand new pair of shoes off the table and slid them on to my feet I realised that it was raining outside, so I opened my umbrella in the atrium and left my castle via the moat. On the way out a black cat ran across my path, so I had to avoid it by ducking under a ladder, this caused me to drop my hand mirror which shattered on all the cracks in the paving slabs that I was stood on.

All the signs were looking positive. I knew I'd be able to complete this challenge.

Suddenly I blacked out. When I awoke I realised that Ian must have drugged me. I knew this, as his whiny voice was informing me saying as much, reverberating around the pitch black room I found myself in, informing me that he had drugged me to whisk me away to the Ultimate Challenge.

The lights in the room flickered on, gently illuminating the shadows around me. I found myself stood on a small podium constructed of pine wood. The wooden platform was elevated above a chasm that seemed to disappear into the bowels of the world. At the bottom of the room I could make out the unmistakable form of a pack of emus darting from left to right in a sinister fashion. Oh, almost forgot to mention, the wooden platform I was stood on was also on fire. The circle of scorching flames surrounding me, searing the skin on my hands as the dancing fire burned ever closer, until both the podium and I would be consumed.

The podium was 20 metres away from the exit, situated on a platform bathed in a faded green light at the far end of the room, the platform balanced precariously on a wooden pole that ran to the ground of the chamber. Between myself and the exit swung Ancient Egyptian Khopseh swords hanging on metals chains, each blade deathly sharp as it swung back and forth. Not only that, but a complex sequence of cannonballs fired from unseen weapons hurtled to and fro in front of my eyes.

Then, there was the Ancient Greek Xiphos swords, which were rotating in a deadly dance of death around the podium, each being propelled by unseen hands. Finally, shuriken's were being sent spinning through the air, dodging between the cannonballs and blades to create an impregnable web of doom between the exit and I.

I stared out across the impossible challenge that Ian had set me.

I recalled everything I had learnt through writing Volume 1 of Escapades in Bizarrchaeology.

And suddenly I knew exactly what I needed to do to survive.

Now clearly I was able to survive (how else could I have written about it otherwise) the question is... can you figure out, based on everything you've read, how I survived the experience? That is your Ultimate Challenge.

Good luck.

Farewell Bizarrchaeologists

Dear person who has been reading this book, I now feel like I know you (even though I have no idea what your name is... Burt? Jeff? Stacy? Falula?). As your sweaty hands have flicked through the pages or clumsily swiped on the screen of your reading device leaving smears in the plastic, I feel we have become close. Very close.

We've been on an adventure together, exploring the ground floor of my Warehouse of Bizarrchaeology and growing both mentally, physically and possibly even spiritually too.

We've learnt of cats who've conquered countries, tanks that look like bicycles and that Vikings wear mascara. We've discovered why you should never be an Adabate gladiator, that emus are more dangerous than tanks and pigeons have what it takes to aim missies.

It's been fun. But time as ever must tick on and I'm afraid it is now time to close the door, lower the portcullis and activate the machine gun nests as the Warehouse of Bizarrchaeology is closed for the day.

But do not fear dear reader, Max Virtus will return. The Warehouse will reopen. And there are far more subterranean depths filled with history of the Bizarre to explore. Until then.

Bibliography

Max Virtus may well have his Warehouse of Bizarrchaeology but Adrian Burrows wouldn't have anything to write about without all of the amazing historians who have shared their discoveries. Thanks to each and every one of you for fuelling my interest in history. It would be impossible to provide a reading list for every book that I've ever read, absorbed random bits into my brain and then regurgitated onto the page (that's a disturbing mental image I'm sure), however, please find below a reading list of some incredible history books from some excellent authors which I'm sure will continue to fuel your passion for history as well.

Ancient Egypt: History in an Hour – Anthony Holmes
A History of Ancient Egypt: From the first farmers to the Great Pyramid – John Romer
Persian Fire – Tom Holland
Eureka! Everything you wanted to know about the Ancient Greeks but were afraid to ask – Peter Jones
The Spartans: An Epic History - Paul Cartledge
Dangerous Days in the Roman Empire – Terry Deary
Gladiator: The Roman Fighter's Unofficial Manuel – Philip Matyszak
Legionary: The Roman Soldier's Unofficial Manuel - Philip Matyszak
SPQR: A Roman Miscellany - Anthony Everitt
Veni Vidi Vici: Everything you wanted to know about the Romans but were afraid to ask – Peter Jones

The Book of Ninja: The Bansenshukai - Anthony Cummins

Samurai: The Japanese Warrior's (Unofficial) Manual - Stephen Turnbull

The Republic of Pirates – Colin Woodward

Uncle John's Bathroom Reader: Plunges into History

Uncle John's Bathroom Reader: Plunges into History Again

A Million Years in a Day – Greg Jenner

History's Worst: 2000 Years of Idiocy – Adam Powell

Viking: The Norse Warrior's (Unofficial) Manual - John Haywood

Over the Top: Great Battles of the First World War - Martin Marix Evans

Horrible Histories – Terry Deary

The Greek Myths – Robin Waterfield

The World at War – Gerard Cheshire

A History of Pirates – Charlotte Montague

Civilisations of the Ancient World – Edited by Professor Dominic Rathbone

Ancient Egypt: Civilisations of the Nile Valley from Pharaohs to Farmers – Parragon Books

30–Second Ancient Rome – Editor Matthew Nicholls

30-Second Ancient Egypt – Editor Peter Der Manuelian

Made in the USA
Charleston, SC
05 November 2016